Blossoming Upward

Blossoming Upward

A Sacred Journey of Transformation

Steven Auerbach

Blossoming Upward by Steven Auerbach

Published by: Nicasio Press
Sebastopol, California
www.nicasiopress.com

ISBN: 979-8-9897756-8-2
Printed in the U.S.A.

To the lineage of Siddha Yoga masters who have awakened the lotus of my heart.

And to my wife, Laura, and my sons, Joel and David, who live at its center.

Honor your Self,
Worship your Self,
Meditate on your Self,
God dwells within you as you.
—Baba Muktananda

Contents

Part Five—Living in Gratitude   187

PREFACE

More than fifty years ago, when I was leaving my guru's ashram in India for the second time, Baba Muktananda said something to me that I will never forget. This siddha, this perfected being, told me that, regarding the human spirit, there are two viewpoints in this world—negative and positive. A person with a negative perspective says, "I am small; I am insignificant," while a person with the true and positive outlook sees that he himself is divine. With this divine vision, Baba said, a person "blossoms upward" in his life.

I understood that he was speaking of the way an individual's consciousness can expand as he goes through his life, moving him toward a recognition of his own true nature.

Blossoming Upward is my account of the spiritual growth that was made possible for me by my association with not one but two enlightened beings. I have had the rare opportunity to spend time with two most extraordinary beings, and this experience has enhanced my life beyond measure. In writing this account, much had to be omitted, of course—it's never possible to convey every single moment, and this book covers some seventy years. The stories contained here are about some of my most memorable experiences. I have changed the names of a few nonpublic figures in order to protect their privacy.

My purpose in writing this book was to share the depth of these experiences. I hope that *Blossoming Upward* provides insight into what it means to be with an enlightened being—and I hope as well that it might inspire the reader to pursue their own spiritual path, however they might conceive it.

PART ONE—AWAKENING

1. Early Life

I feel like my life actually began in the fall of 1969. I was twenty years old at the time. I was lying in bed at my parents' house reading *The Hobbit* by J.R.R. Tolkien. My mind was absorbed in the book. Suddenly and unexpectedly, my inner awareness was drawn upward, and above my head a sun appeared. It was covered with clouds that were just beginning to clear away. As the clouds parted, this sun grew brighter and brighter. I sat up with a gasp, and, in an instantaneous flash, I experienced with remarkable clarity that the entire universe was the infinite body of God. This was not a thought I had ever had before. In fact, it wasn't a thought at all. It was something else entirely. It was an explosion of a new perception of myself and the world.

I'd had no religious or philosophical training to prepare me for this. I felt like I had awakened from a dream to a new reality. Everything I had ever thought about myself was suddenly new. It changed everything, and I have never been the same since. I thought it was a final transformation. I didn't know it was just the beginning of an amazing journey. I wanted more!

I was on fire with this awareness. I had no way of interpreting this experience and had no foundation with which to put any of it into a context. I tried to share this excitement with some of my friends. "Have you read Alan Watts?" one of my friends asked me. "He says the same thing."

Actually, I had not read any philosophical writings. All I knew was that I had to understand what had just happened to me and that I felt so alive.

In retrospect, I can see that I'd had life experiences that had prepared me for what was beginning to unfold.

*   *   *

My family was liberal, socially responsible, culturally Jewish, but not religious. I grew up with values that taught me to try to make the world a better place. I was the fourth of five children, with three older brothers and a younger sister. The person I was closest to in our family was my mother. The earliest memory I can recall is of being with my mother at a "Ban the Bomb" rally across the street from the United Nations Headquarters in New York City. I would have been five or six years old.

Pete Seeger was there, standing on a wooden crate and accompanied by his banjo. He was singing "Ain't Gonna Study War No More" with a small crowd of perhaps twenty-five people. Somehow, that memory has stayed with me. I saw him many times over the years to come. I would say Pete Seeger was one of my heroes. I felt his humanity, intelligence, and compassion, and I tried to hold on to those qualities in my life.

As a very young child, I remember that I was happy. It's a vivid memory; it seemed that everywhere I went, strangers would ask me, "Why are you so happy?" I think I noticed this because it happened so often. I must have just smiled a lot. I remember telling my older brother, Ted, that when I grew up, I wanted to be a clown because it seemed that people weren't happy. I thought that must be why people always asked me why I was happy.

Ted told me, "You can't be a clown! You'd have to travel with a circus, and you'd never see your family!"

"OK," I told him, "then I'll be a doctor. If I can't make people happy, at least I can make them well."

*   *   *

As I got older, I was inspired by many of the peace demonstrations in New York and Washington, DC, that took place when I was in my teens. I was physically present when Martin Luther King gave his famous "I Have a Dream" speech on August 28, 1963. That day there were over 250,000 people marching for a more equitable, more just society. "Jobs and Freedom" the signs and placards said. The sense of solidarity was palpable. Blacks and whites were marching together for a better world. When I was much younger, I'd told my mother that I never understood why everyone had to be thought of as black or white when we were actually all brown and pink.

When I was in my teens in the mid and late sixties, the Vietnam War was raging. Whenever I could, I went to the anti-war rallies that were taking place. These were tumultuous times, but I felt inspired to be standing up for what I truly believed. I have always felt that violence has no place in a peace demonstration. It didn't happen often, but there were times when I was too close to more aggressive activities and found myself in a crowd of people who got tear gassed. This is an experience I would not like to repeat. Still, I felt I needed to be there.

One day when I was about fifteen, I remember coming out of a New York City subway station on my way to a demonstration downtown. That day there had been talk that the opposition facing us might be violent. I remember feeling some fear about going and yet thinking to myself, as I tightened the belt on my jacket, that I had to be there. I had to speak up.

If not me, then who?

2. College Years

My father, a New York City taxi driver, encouraged me to go to a college out of town. I would have been happy to leave New York, and I applied to the University of Hawaii—the farthest point from "the familiar" that I could think of. I was accepted at the UH, but in the end, there was no money to support my going so far away. It was up to me to pay for college, so I started my college studies at Queensborough Community College in Queens, New York.

Sometime in my second year at Queensboro, I was approached by a classmate, who wanted me to attend a meeting of the Students for a Democratic Society—SDS. I didn't know much about the SDS and wasn't much interested at first. After some prodding, I agreed to go. There, I found a group of about twenty-five students discussing social issues and the seeming apathy of the student body. They were looking for ways to raise the political consciousness of the campus. It seemed to me that they were sincere but inexperienced. At some point I spoke up regarding some thoughts I had. I don't remember a word of what I said. What I didn't know was that they were holding an election that day for officers of the club. Out of left field, someone nominated me for president. I left that meeting stunned that I had just become president of the local chapter of the SDS. I remember going home and telling my mother what had happened and the shock on her face was quite evident. I was generally the quieter one in the family when it came to political action.

*   *   *

At the very next meeting, there was a guest who had previously been invited to speak. He was Dr. Donald Silberman, a professor at the college, who was being let go for espousing his political views. He was a leftist and a member of the Progressive Labor Party. I wasn't terribly impressed by him, but this was a question of free speech involving a man who was generally well thought of by his students and colleagues. I saw it as a solid civil liberties issue that could bring to light some of the broader political issues of the day.

Our group began a free speech campaign on the campus to protect Dr. Silberman's right to hold his own views; we demanded his reinstatement. We had the support of a number of faculty and department chairmen as well as many other student organizations.

As this progressed, on April 16, 1969, we held a rally on the front lawn of the college. A lot of people came. There were a few faculty and student speakers, and then, as I was president of the SDS chapter as well as chairman of the ad-hoc coalition in charge of this demonstration, I was the final speaker. As planned, I called for a sit-in to take place on the fourth floor of the administration building, which was the largest building on campus and which held the offices of the college president, many of his deans, and the secretarial staff, as well as a large, open common area. About twelve hundred demonstrators—students and faculty—followed me into the building. This was the first time in my life that I realized I had a voice.

The Queensboro president, Dr. Kurt Schmeller, was twenty-nine when he became president of QCC in 1966, which was very young for this position. At the time, I think he was the youngest college president in the country. Dr. Schmeller's focus for his PhD had been German economic theory, and the swastikas that adorned some of the bindings of books on the shelf in his office didn't do much to endear him to any of us.

I was leading the group as we approached the staircase to the fourth floor. Standing at the top of the stairs was President Schmeller and two of his deans, their arms folded in front of them, effectively blocking our way forward. It was reminiscent of Alabama Governor

George Wallace's stance in blocking of the University of Alabama auditorium in 1963 to prevent the enrollment of African American students. I don't know where the idea came from, but without a conscious thought, I ran back outside and entered the building again through a lower door. I came up the stairs behind President Schmeller, stepping between him and his dean as I said, "Excuse me." I then opened the way for the other students to enter. To Schmeller's great surprise, all twelve hundred did.

*   *   *

This was an interesting time within the New York higher educational system. Students were holding sit-ins at many of the city colleges and universities. At Queensborough, however, we were uniquely creative. As we congregated in the common area for the next two weeks, we never asked the administrative staff to leave the building. The staff were able to continue with all their normal functions. We held our activities around them. Also, we never prevented students from going to classes. We stayed in the administration building day and night. We took up collections for our food—and fed the security guards as well. Jack Goodman, the head of security, had locked himself in the president's office to protect it. We would knock on his door and make sure he was taken care of. I had great concern that our sit-in remained peaceful.

There were many speeches and discussions during this time. With the help of a few professors, who shared their contacts, we invited many well-known speakers and musicians to provide information and entertainment. I wish I could remember all the notable speakers and guests. Among them, I do recall, was Joseph Heller, author of the book *Catch 22*. Heller did a reading from his book. Herschel Bernardi, the actor who played Tevya in the Broadway musical *Fiddler on the Roof*, came and—to everyone's delight—sang "If I Were a Rich Man." This was the only time that all the secretaries and administrative staff left their desks and came out of their offices to listen.

After two weeks, the demonstration became routine and so— unfortunately—not as effective. A group of the key demonstrators got together and decided we had to step up this protest to a full lockdown of the administrative building.

The next morning, after we'd allowed all the college staff to enter as usual, we announced that we were shutting down the building. Speaking very politely, we asked them to leave, which they did. We then announced to the students and faculty who were participating in this sit-in that any of them who wished to leave could do so as well. A number did go. After that, we barricaded the entrance to the fourth floor.

It wasn't long after this that we could see, as we watched from the rooftop, that riot squads and police cars were quietly lining up just outside the four main gates of the campus. As the police got out of their transport vehicles, we could see that some of them were in riot gear and were banging their batons on their hands, clearly ready for a fight. I had the notion that we should get creative again. We watched and waited for them to make their move. Suddenly, they came onto the campus with full force, simultaneously from all four gates. My plan was to wait for the police to advance and then have everyone leave, quickly and unseen, by a side door. This worked beautifully. To the great surprise of the police, when they got there, they found the building was empty!

We then all then returned the next morning and retook the building.

That next day, the drama was repeated. This time, however, an ultra-conservative campus group known as the Young Americans for Freedom tried to block the doors to the admin building so that we couldn't get out. I heard that the YAF crowd was particularly looking for me. We pushed our way through and made it out. Jack, another student, and I were the last two to leave the building. I had insisted on being the last out to make sure everyone else made it out safely. When Jack and I emerged from the building, there was a shout: "There's Auerbach! Get him!" They pounced. I managed to escape without harm, but, in the confusion, Jack wasn't so lucky. That afternoon, I found out that he had been beaten badly enough to break his arm.

That night about twenty-five of us held a secret meeting at a nearby residence to plan our next step. At least we had thought it was a secret meeting. While we were there, this place—someone's home—was raided by uniformed and plainclothes officers. It turns out that one of our regular sit-in students was an undercover policeman and had informed on us. That night, we were all arrested and booked. After spending a night in jail, we were released, pending a hearing.

*   *   *

A few weeks later, there were separate hearings for each of the civil and criminal charges. In the civil case, we were represented by lawyers from the American Civil Liberties Union, including Martin Garbus, who later was recognized as one of the leading first amendment lawyers in the country. The charge in the criminal proceedings was criminal trespass, and for that we were represented by Moe Tandler, a prominent civil rights attorney. The result was that nine of us who were the leaders of the sit-in were given fifteen-day sentences on notorious Rikers Island—the largest correctional institution in New York City and one of the largest in the entire country.

Rikers Island was a thought-provoking experience. It had a population of about ten thousand men, most of them being held for pre-trial hearings because they couldn't afford to post bail. Some of these men had been on Rikers Island for years. While my cohorts and I were there, we had some interesting conversations with the other inmates. Quite a few of these men told us that they had honed their criminal skills while in jail. Many others—I would say most—claimed to be innocent.

We began to lead political discussions during common times outside of our two-man cells. We were all subsequently released after nine days for "good behavior."

Later, at a presidential hearing at Queensboro, we were all expelled from school.

My father commented on all of this only after he began receiving letters from complete strangers, criticizing him for my behavior. Articles on the demonstrations had been running in the *Long Island Daily Press*, including a photo of me and some of the other demonstrators being booked at the local police station. People were sending my father bible tracts and nasty comments. He was mildly amused by this. My mother took it all very well. She told me that she was proud that I was standing up for something I believed in. She may have been concerned, but she always backed me up.

3. Evolution

For the first time in my life, I found myself with no responsibilities, no schedules to attend to, and no particular plans for my future. It was very freeing, but there was also uncertainty as to what would come next. I spent a lot of time hanging out in the student lounge of Queens College, a large city university, where I had a lot of friends. I was ripe for a new adventure.

One sunny afternoon as I was walking in a nearby park with my friend Phil, we stopped to rest on the lawn. While we were sitting, a very old woman who was being pushed in a wheelchair by her attendant stopped on the path, got up, and approached us. There was something about this woman that was strikingly radiant. Speaking softly, she said to us, "I'd like to tell you about time, space, and eternity." She handed us each a pamphlet with a Christian message. This woman was so sweet and sincere that she made an impression on me. The next day, I was thinking about her, and I began to wonder, "What if she's right?" I'd had no exposure to religious thought. What if I was missing something vital? For the first time in my life, I actually knelt down next to my bed and prayed: "God, if there's anything to this, please show me." After that I let it all go and didn't really think about it again.

It was about two months later, when I was relaxing in bed and reading *The Hobbit*, that it all happened. I had a sudden vision above my head. I saw clouds parting to reveal a sun, and this was followed by a dynamic flash of understanding that the entire universe was itself the physical form of God. It wasn't that there *is* a God; it was that it is *all* God!

*   *   *

Some months passed. I wanted to pursue a deepening of this experience, but I didn't have a clue as to how I could do that. Sometime in early December of 1969, a few friends of mine were going to visit our friend Gary in Norman, Texas. His family had a cabin in the mountains of Eagles Nest, New Mexico, which was about eighty miles from Taos Ski Valley. Our plan was to ski there.

The high desert town of Taos is about a mile south of Taos Pueblo, a community of multi-story adobe dwellings built somewhere between 1000 and 1450 AD. The home of the Pueblo people, this is one of the oldest continuously inhabited settlements in North America.

As we stopped in the central square of the town of Taos, I stepped out of the car facing Mount Wheeler, which locally is referred to as Mount Taos and is considered sacred to the native Americans who live there. I looked up when suddenly a visible beam of energy, which looked like a cartoon radio wave, came off the mountaintop and smacked me hard on my forehead. I heard a voice that said, "Come back!" Amazed, I turned around and saw a young man who was crossing the opposite side of the square and carrying a large sign with big red letters that had originally read, REVOLUTION. The first R had a diagonal line through it, and so the sign now read, EVOLUTION. It seemed to me that the universe was giving me clues I could not ignore.

*   *   *

After this trip I went back to New York as soon as I could, packed a bag, and returned to Taos. My friend Gary thought it would be a great adventure, and he decided to join me.

At that time in the Taos area, there were a number of communes where people had been experimenting with new ways of living. Gary and I settled in at a place called the Five Star Ranch.

It had already had its day, and by this point the ranch had been pretty much abandoned as a commune. However, there were still about twenty-five people living there, mostly just passing through. The ranch had a large natural pool that was fed by hot springs. This was the middle of the New Mexican winter. The temperatures at night were well below zero, and relaxing in the 110-degree water of this spring-fed pool was a heavenly experience. One evening at sunset, we were in the hot spring just as the sun was setting. The sky turned a glorious red and orange as a gentle snow began to fall. Magical!

It was around this time that I met Tatha. He was a few years older than me, and he had been practicing yoga for some time. Tatha took a liking to me, and we spent a lot of time talking about spirituality. He was the first person who understood what I was experiencing. I valued his insights and understanding. He taught me some basic yoga postures and put me on a ten-day cleansing brown rice diet. Later, I learned his real name was Marvin Glover from Florida.

We stayed in Taos for about a month. During this time, a group of Vietnam war veterans were passing through. These vets were an engaging crew of musicians and storytellers with great tales to tell, and we all became friends. They were on their way to Hawaii, where they had plans to meet up with a few others and establish a commune on Maui. It was very cold where we were, and Hawaii sounded like a great idea. Gary and I were invited to join them, and so we did. Tatha came with us.

4. MAUI

We drove to San Francisco. After spending a few days in the Haight-Ashbury District near Golden Gate Park, a few others joined us. By the time we took off for Hawaii, there were about eight of us. I didn't have much money. I arrived in Hawaii with only fifteen dollars in my pocket. I just knew that this was where I needed to be. On Maui, we were met at the Kahalui Airport by a friend, who drove us out to Makena Beach.

I stepped out onto the beautiful, silky, white-sand beach and, as if right on cue, was greeted by a large marlin jumping fully out of the water. Right behind it, a whale breached as well. Then the marlin jumped again, followed once more by the whale. This magical succession between the huge fish and the marine mammal must have been repeated at least five times as they playfully traversed the lagoon in front of us just a few hundred yards offshore. I felt like I was in heaven.

I lived on Makena Beach for the next month, bathing in the ocean, doing some daily yoga postures, eating sparsely, meditating, and reading a miniature bible that I carried with me.

One morning, I was sitting close to the shore, looking through *The Complete Illustrated Book of Yoga* by Swami Vishnudevananda. A friend on the beach had been reading this book, and I borrowed it from him for an hour or so. It was the first book on yoga I had ever seen. As I read it, I became aware that two spirit beings had walked over and stood next to me. They were male, tall, and had beautiful golden tan bodies. They wore only loincloths. Their skulls were an interesting shape—very slightly elongated. They were clearly benign and were looking at the book I held with great curiosity, from over my shoulder. One of them kneeled down to get a better look at it. I turned the book slightly toward him so he could see it more easily. The two of them stayed a few moments, and then I could no longer see them. Looking back at this, I think that I was just so open to this new life and an expanded spirituality that these beings became visible to me. It felt like a very natural experience.

*   *   *

Within a few days of our arrival on Maui, it had become clear that our traveling group had diverse ideas about where and how to set up a community. Very soon, we went our separate ways, agreeing to meet at the top of Haleakala Crater at the next full moon.

Maui is the second largest of the Hawaiian Islands and was formed by two volcanoes. The largest of these is Haleakala, the mountain that makes up the bulk of the island. Over 10,023 feet above sea level, Haleakala is one of the largest dormant volcanoes in the world. At the top, the crater is huge: about 7.5 miles across, 2.5 miles wide, and almost three thousand feet deep. Haleakala is so large that there are many cinder cones within it, making for an extraordinary view from the top. It has been considered a sacred site by the local Hawaiians for more than a thousand years.

As my original group of friends had planned to meet at the next full moon, I left the beach a few days early to meet them at our agreed upon meeting time on the summit of Haleakala Crater. The road that leads to the summit is thirty-six miles of hairpin turns—the longest road in the world going the shortest distance. I was easily able to hitchhike a ride to the top. The scenic views on the road are incredible. You go from sea level with the expected tropical flora, to pine and eucalyptus forests as it climbs higher into the cloud layer at about 8,000 feet. Then it rises above the clouds with only sparse vegetation and finally to the top which looks reminiscent of another planet with its muted tones of rust and grey.

As it turned out, I was the only one of our original group to show up. After waiting for some time, I decided to descend into the crater alone on the marked Sliding Sands Trail. I had only an apple and a small box of raisins with me.

After descending for twenty minutes or so, I stopped when I saw the figure of a small boy running past me smiling playfully and joyfully. His skin was a slightly greenish color. He was dressed only in a lavalava, a short cloth wrapped around his waist. He quickly vanished. Months later I learned of the traditional Hawaiian tales of the Menehune, a race of small people who are said to live in the deep forests and hidden valleys of Hawaii. Had I just seen a Menehune? I wouldn't know how else to explain it. I simply said, "Hello," and continued on.

It's about a five hour walk to the crater floor, and it was getting a bit dark and colder, so I stopped to rest for the night. When I awoke the next morning there was a light fog around me. I then saw a beautiful rainbow. Its beautiful curves ended about ten feet on either side of me. "Ahh," I thought, "the pot of gold at the end of the rainbow! It was my own self. That's where the treasure is found." Years later, I learned that the full rainbow is actually a complete circle, usually only seen from above, as in an airplane. So, the pot of gold has no beginning or end and is all around us, if only we knew how to look. I continued on, for about another five hours across the crater floor.

On the far side of the crater, I met a group of people who had rented one of the three cabins within the crater. Their cabin sat on the top of the Kaupo Gap, where a trail begins that descends down to the sea. I spent the night with them and set out in the morning for what I expected was to be a final five-hour hike down the Kaupo Gap.

The trail was quite sparse, and after an hour or so, I realized I had lost the trail. I tried to backtrack, but I couldn't find the trail, so I decided to continue downward. I figured that as long as I was heading downhill, I would eventually get to the bottom.

After walking a while, I found myself facing a patch of dense thorny bushes that stood about seven feet high. Going around this barrier didn't seem possible, and it didn't make sense to turn back. I felt I had no choice other than to go through them. I began to claw my way through the thorns inch by inch. I was already exhausted, and I hadn't eaten in three days. Within moments, I was all scratched up and was in survival mode. I had to get through this. The temperature was very hot, easily ninety degrees or more. I was thirsty and yet realized the small bolo of water I carried had fallen off somewhere in the thorns. Things were getting worse. At one point I fell down exhausted and realized that if I rested there, I could pass out, become unconscious and no one would ever find me. I picked myself up and continued on.

Suddenly I heard the bleating of a goat. There are small herds of goats that live in the crater. I couldn't see this goat, but he kept bleating. I followed his sound and soon found a small trail about two feet high that the goats used to move through the thick brush. I crawled through that trail on my hands and knees following the constant sound of the goat. I never did see him, but I think he saved my life.

On the other side of that brush was a small puddle of water with a yellow flower growing alongside it. I realized that it would not be best to drink from that puddle, but I felt it was a blessing and I did take a few sips—fortunately, to no harm.

As I continued, I felt I couldn't stay on a straight downward path anymore, so I decided to cross over toward the opposite side of the gap. The terrain became more open, and I came upon an old, hardened lava flow that was heading downward. This was solid smooth rock, and I was able to walk along it for some time unrestricted until I encountered a significant drop of about fifteen feet. There seemed to be nowhere else to go. But then I noticed a thin ledge—about six inches wide—that moved along the side of the drop, angling downward. By walking on this ledge, I might be able to get far enough down that I could jump to the bottom. With my back to the wall, I inched my way carefully. About halfway across I looked below and saw the decaying carcass of a goat that had obviously tried the same route I was taking—and hadn't made it. I had to keep going. Finally, I was able to jump six feet down to the ground.

I kept walking until I came to another very steep drop. This one was more than twenty feet down. This time, there was no alternative route down. I realized I would have to change direction. The walls surrounding me were perhaps fifteen feet high, and I needed to climb them to get out of the lava flow. The sides were mostly loose dirt with some sparse vegetation.

I began to climb. It was a very steep incline, almost straight up. I was grabbing at loosely anchored vegetation for support. At one point, while I was hanging on to a plant, I swung my right foot over to a hole in the ground for a foothold. It turned out to be a beehive. Hundreds of bees suddenly swarmed and were bouncing all over me. Amazingly, not one stung me. I slid down about ten feet and waited for the bees to settle down. I still had to pass them to continue upward. I was very careful as I went by them. Fortunately, they didn't bother me.

I then came out onto a hillside, which I walked on until it began to get dark. I was in the midst of a lot of small trees and brush. The visibility was poor, so I decided to stop for my third night, without food or drink in the crater.

I lay down and slept a short while until I was awakened by some clomping noises very close to me. I looked up and perhaps five feet away, was a path and a group of cows walking on it. I lay still, and they didn't notice me. Afterward, I went back to sleep. When I awoke, I continued on my journey through the light brush.

A bit later I came upon an open field where a herd of cattle was grazing. When they saw me, the cows turned and ran, and that left one very large bull. He stood maybe twenty-five feet in front of me as he lowered his head slightly. I just stared at him, matching his intensity. I HAD to go that way. There was no turning back. We locked eyes for a few long moments. There wasn't a sound. We both were totally and completely still. Then I suddenly threw my arms up in the air and yelled "Yaaaahh!!!" The bull turned and took off running. I felt bad about scaring him like that. I yelled out, "Sorry!"

as he ran off. It could only have been the intensity of the prior few days that allowed me to confront him that way.

Finally, I crossed the field and came down onto a dirt road that was so bumpy and gutted that rented vehicles were forbidden to drive on it. I was about six miles from Hana, the nearest town. By road, going around the perimeter of the island, I was about eighty miles from my starting point on the opposite end of the crater.

Not many people drove on this section of road, and I began the six-mile hike toward Hana thinking that I'd be walking most of the way. After just a few minutes, a rare passing car stopped for me. In it were two Canadian women; the driver asked if I needed a lift. Yes, I did! She said she wouldn't normally have stopped for anyone, but I reminded her of her son who was about the same age. After ten minutes or so, she asked me if I had eaten lunch. She was quite surprised when I told her I hadn't eaten in four days and had been lost up on the Kaupo Gap.

We drove on into Hana, and she stopped at the Hana Ranch Store. She sent me inside and said, "Get everything you want—as much as you want." She loaded up four or five grocery bags of food for me, and the three of us went out to the nearby Hana Beach, where the women spread a blanket, and we had a feast. They then drove me all the way around the island to a house where I knew I could stay for a while. I was left with enough groceries to last for two weeks.

I think I must have lost about ten pounds during my ordeal. It was transformative, as survival experiences can be. I was aware of my mind being totally clear. I felt open to whatever new adventures were to come.

*   *   *

Over the next few months, I began visiting different spiritual groups on the island. I wanted to understand their experiences of their faith. I loved chanting with the devotees at the Haiku Meditation Center and spent a lot of time there. I usually had

Sunday lunch at the Huelo Door of Faith Church in Huelo and had a full water baptism there one weekend. I went to a few meetings with those of the Baha'i faith. I visited Buddhist temples. Everywhere I went, I wanted to know what they believed and what their personal experiences were. What was their concept of God?

I began to see that all of these groups were trying to reach similar states of connection with their particular concept of divinity. I was still experiencing profound states of awareness of the daily presence of God that were deepening in me as I observed all of these different paths, shared my understanding, and made many friends. I saw the commonalities as well as the cultural and theological differences between all of these groups.

I most often walked to these places, usually miles in between. I would just walk along the roads enjoying the moment, feeling very full. Sometimes a car would stop and someone would offer a lift, sometimes not. Sometimes I had food, sometimes not. Often, I intentionally fasted for three days at a time. A few times, I fasted for a full seven days, taking only water and tea. Sometimes, I would pick a fragrant flower—these are quite abundant in Hawaii—and while smelling it, I would feel all my senses being satisfied. I would feel no hunger. I loved being out on the open road.

One day, when I was walking along a quiet back road, I suddenly felt as if I were walking a foot off the ground. I was surrounded by a soft sparkling light. I looked down and saw myself in the body of an old man with a long white beard. I was wearing simple white robes and holding a walking stick. This experience felt quite natural and lasted for a few minutes. Was this a glimpse into a past life? When I look back and reflect on those days, it seems clear that I was in a profound state of grace.

Some weeks later, I met a man who had recently returned from India. He had been a swami, an Indian monk, and had recently stepped away from that role. His monastic name had been Swami Brahmananda, and he had been in the Bihar ashram of Swami Satyananda, who was a disciple of Swami Sivananda, the founder of the Divine Life Society. This man, who was from the Bronx, was known then as Eddie. At that time, on Maui, we mostly called him Swami Eddie.

I was fascinated by Swami Eddie's stories of discipleship and India, and I spent about two weeks traveling around Maui with him. He shared many insights and understandings that I really resonated with. It became clear that the next step for me was on the horizon. I had to get to India somehow.

*   *   *

It was around this time that I received a notice that I was to appear in Honolulu at the local draft board for induction into the Army. This was 1970, and the Vietnam war was still going strong. I had lost my student deferment from the military when I left college. I was flown at government expense from Maui to Honolulu and was put up at the local YMCA along with thirty or so other men. On the flight over, there was a young man dressed only in a lavalava, the short Hawaiian skirt. He had long hair, no shirt, and was decked out with strings of beads. He carried only a wooden flute. When we arrived at the draft board, I heard the sound of his flute and looked up to see that he had climbed a large banyan tree and was sitting in the branches. He obviously wanted to demonstrate that he wasn't fit for military service. It turned out that he had seven letters from psychiatrists confirming this.

Emboldened by this fellow, I told the recruiters that I simply didn't want to go. While waiting in line, I closed my eyes to meditate for a moment and quite unexpectedly saw the image of the head of Jesus appear…somewhat unusual for a nice Jewish boy from New York. Projecting from his forehead was the figure of a small dark man, dressed in orange with his head cocked to one side, looking at me with a sly smile. I was subsequently released without conscription.

This was the last obstacle to my going to India—although I had no money. I had arrived on Maui seven months prior with just fifteen dollars in my pocket. I still had five dollars of the original fifteen. During my time there, I slept on beaches and ate fruits that I could pick myself or food that was shared with me by the various people I met. As a choice, I had fasted frequently. The fasting was cleansing, and it energized me. I was the healthiest I had ever been in my life.

The very next day, I met a man who was looking for people to help him work on roofing jobs he had lined up. He was installing cedar shingle roofing, which is common in Hawaii. He offered to train me and to pay me quite well. After eight days I had enough airfare to fly back to New York, where I had left four hundred dollars in a bank account. This was the last money I had to my name.

One of my friends from Hawaii, Jonathan, who had also spent time with Swami Eddie, wanted to come with me to India. We'd planned to meet in New York and then travel together to Bihar State, India, to meet Swami Eddie's guru. After I arrived in New York, Jonathan called to tell me he had broken his leg in a motorcycle accident. He suggested I go on to India alone and that we meet up later.

I stayed at my parent's house for a bit to figure out my next step.

5. Return to New York

During this time in New York, I sometimes went into Manhattan and just walked. One day as I was walking in lower Manhattan, I came upon a Krishna Temple that was serving a free lunch feast. I always loved their chanting on Maui, so I went inside. In fact, I had come across them some years earlier in 1966, while I was in high school. At that time, I was visiting my eldest brother, George, who lived on Second Avenue on the Lower East Side. As I walked, I heard the sound of tinkling cymbals from the other side of the street. The sound intrigued me, so I crossed the street to check it out. There were a few young men on the sidewalk, handing out small, mimeographed sheets that said simply, "Stay high forever! Chant these words," followed by the words of their mantra: *Hare Krishna Hare Krishna, Krishna Krishna Hare Hare, Hare Rama Hare Rama, Rama Rama Hare Hare.* This was before the group had become well known. In fact, this was their first center in the U.S.

I knew nothing about them; I went inside out of curiosity. Their teacher, Srila Prabhupada, who was the founder of their movement, was there, and we chanted together—quite sweetly—for twenty minutes or so. They also passed around some sweets. I felt unusually happy there. Afterward, when I told my mother about the experience, she expressed concern. She said, "Maybe they put something in the food." But I knew it was the chanting.

I knew nothing about their philosophy, but I knew the chanting felt good, so I would sometimes chant their mantra to myself. I don't think I actually knew the word "mantra" at the time, I just liked the sounds. One day, while I was home alone after school, I began chanting this mantra. Unexpectedly, the image of a small blue being appeared in front of me, seated in a yoga posture. I didn't even know the word "yoga" back then, and the experience of seeing this benevolent being frightened me a bit. I didn't know what to make of it. I had no context for understanding it. I just stopped saying that mantra entirely and completely forgot all about the whole experience.

A few years later, one of my older brothers, Paul, actually joined the Hare Krishna movement. He became the personal valet to Srila Prabhupada—whose formal name was A.C. Bhaktivedanta Swami Prabhupada—and traveled the world with him in that capacity for several years.

So, now, in 1970, I was having lunch at the Krishna Center sitting on the floor next to an older woman, who had a few students around her and was having an interesting discussion with them about spiritual matters. She invited me to a meditation session with her group at an apartment on the Upper West Side.

This woman was Hilda Charlton. She was a beautiful teacher, and she shared many stories of her time in India. She had gone there on a dance tour in 1947 and stayed in India for about fifteen years. During that time, she visited with numerous holy men. She was very taken with Bhagavan Nityananda of Ganeshpuri, whom she visited frequently. She was also fond of Sai Baba of Puttaparthi, known as Sathya Sai Baba. In later years, Hilda became very popular in New York—more than a thousand people would come to her meetings, which eventually moved to the Cathedral of St. John the Divine in uptown Manhattan.

I spent a few weeks going to sessions in her apartment, and I was always uplifted by her presence. One day I told her that I wanted to delay my trip to India by a few more months so that I could save more money for the journey.

She said, "That's great. Then you can meet Muktananda when he comes."

Having never heard of this Muktananda, I asked, "Who's that?"

She said, "Nityananda became Muktananda. And Nityananda was God. So, you should think that God is coming to New York."

Well, I wasn't going to pass up on a chance to meet God! So, that confirmed the delay of my travel plans. To earn money, I took a job driving a New York City taxicab for a few months.

During this interim time, I was introduced to and spent time with Baba Ram Dass and spent a few weekends at his father's property in Franklin, New Hampshire, where Ram Dass would hold retreats. I also spent time with Murshid Sam Lewis, known as Sufi Sam, who came to New York around that time. Sufi Sam was quite the eccentric; he taught circle dances that he received in dreams. I danced with him in Central Park and in private homes. One day at an apartment in Brooklyn, he stopped the dance, and, speaking directly to me, he said, "I can see you have come to this earth to help bring in the new age. That's so obvious to me, it ain't even funny." That's the way Sufi Sam talked. He was from California, but he talked like a lot of New Yorkers do.

I was so wide open then that I just took in his words. I figured it was true for us all.

1970: This is the photo I had taken for my visa to India, after my return to New York City from Maui and just before my meeting Swami Muktananda. I was twenty-one.

PART TWO—TRANSFORMATION

6. MEETING BABA, 1970

Finally, the time came to meet Baba Muktananda. He arrived in New York on Wednesday September 3, 1970. On Friday, September 5, a few carloads of us from Hilda's group—including Nandini Weitzman and Gauri Hubert—were traveling upstate to Big Indian, New York, where Baba was holding the first of four weekend retreats. Our caravan stopped at a gas station on the New York Thruway. On the way back to our car from the restroom, some of us saw a station wagon pull up to the gas pump. It was being driven by Michael, a student of Rudi's. Rudi was the one who owned the Big Indian property where the retreats were being held and who had paid for Baba's tour by providing around-the-world airline tickets for Baba and the handful of people who traveled with him.

Sitting in the front passenger seat of this station wagon was Baba. He was listening to an eight-track stereo recording of the Beatles. I love that it was the *Magical Mystery Tour* album. Baba greeted us with love. He opened the car's glove compartment and pulled out a Mr. Goodbar chocolate bar. He broke it in pieces and passed them out to us, waved, and said, "We'll meet soon," and then drove off.

This was the first of four retreats at Big Indian. In these retreats, Baba spoke multiple times a day. He was available throughout the day and sat out with us after lunch, when we would chant with great enthusiasm. I was enthralled by him. He exuded an indescribable energy that was absolutely palpable. After the outdoor chant that followed lunch, Baba and everyone went to rest. I just wanted to sit where he sat. Each day I would sit in the red metal lawn chair he always used and meditated in it for a while. I felt like I was soaking up his energy.

I was quite the novice and had no understanding of Indian etiquette. On a small porch of the dining area, there was a large, cushioned chair that Baba sometimes used when meeting people privately. It looked quite comfortable to me, and I thought it must also have great energy. I sat down and meditated there for a short while. After a few moments, I became aware that someone was sitting next to me. It was Papa Trivedi, the brother of Baba's secretary (Pratibha Trivedi whom we called Amma), who were both traveling on tour with Baba. Speaking very sweetly, this middle-aged Indian man said, "Great vibrations, huh?"

I told him, "Yes, it's really amazing. Everywhere he sits, you can feel his energy."

Papa acknowledged this and very calmly explained that because of that, his seat is kept especially for him.

I will always appreciate Papa's calm, understanding manner. There was no admonition or scolding. He was just letting me know. Of course, I learned from this.

*   *   *

Back in New York City, on weekdays between the four weekend retreats at Big Indian, Baba resided at Rudi's meditation center on the Lower East Side of Manhattan, on Tenth Street between Third and Fourth Avenues. *Satsangs*, chants, and meditation sessions were held in a large hall on the ground floor that held about a hundred people. You could meditate with Baba in the early mornings, and every evening he would give a talk to a full house. Most of the people around him at that time were students of Hilda, Baba Ram Dass, or Rudi.

Baba would give an engrossing talk on the benefits and the more esoteric aspects of meditation, and then this would be followed by an informal question and answer session. I attended both sessions every day, and I also went to all four retreats on the weekends.

One evening I was listening to his lecture when quite suddenly I could no longer see Baba's physical form. My eyes were fully open, but all I could see in the place where he should have been sitting was a mass of blue light. I was quite surprised at this. I turned around then to look at the people in the room behind me. I could clearly see a beautiful ray of blue light emanating from Baba that was entering the chest of every person in the room. I looked down at myself and saw the same ray of light entering me.

Perceiving this ray of light, my vision became introverted. I was drawn inward, and I became totally absorbed in that light. I saw, felt, and perceived deeply that I was that light. From this experience, I understood that this was Baba's message. He was not there to show us his state and his greatness but to show us ours. That is the message of a true Siddha, an enlightened being. The ability to transmit or awaken that awareness in us is the role of a true Guru.

And I observed that so many were awakened in Baba's presence.

*   *   *

One day, following the early meditation—which, as I recall, began around 5:30 a.m.—I had the desire to meditate longer. When I finally got up to leave, I realized that I was alone. Everyone else had already left. When I got to the door of the meditation room, I found that it was locked from the outside. I knocked quite a few times, but no one responded. I wasn't really concerned and just sat back down to meditate more. I stayed in that room all day until someone came to prepare the room for that evening's satsang. It was late in the afternoon. This young man was quite surprised to find that I had been there all day.

I, however, had had a peaceful and relaxing day, meditating and napping. No worries.

One morning after the early meditation, Baba took a walk around the neighborhood with Jinendra Jain—called Professor Jain —who was his translator at the time. A woman named Kali and I followed behind them. When we returned to the meditation center

Baba sat on the front stoop. He asked me who I was and what my plans were.

I told him that I was preparing to go to India.

Baba said, "Yes, go right to the Ganeshpuri Ashram. I'll give you a letter of introduction. When I get there, you can be my driver, and we will travel together all over India." Of course, I was thrilled with this and looked forward to it with great excitement.

On the last day of the last Big Indian Retreat, there was a particularly ecstatic chant after lunch. This was the final chant of the retreat, and everyone chanted with great enthusiasm. When the chant concluded, people dispersed to rest. A few of us wanted to chant more, and in an excess of devotion, we sat just outside Baba's room, continuing to chant enthusiastically.

Amma came out and said we needed to be quiet as Baba was resting. Carried by the emotion of the moment, we didn't listen and continued our chanting. My eyes were closed when I saw a column of white light walk into the room. I opened my eyes and saw that it was Baba. He walked behind us to the far-left corner of the room. I instinctively jumped up and ran to him, bowing at his feet. At that moment I felt myself being lifted up into a timeless state that felt ancient. There were only the two of us. I didn't know if I was on earth. Baba then touched each of my outstretched hands with his right foot, and each time he did so, I saw, heard, and felt, with a loud click, a clear blue spark entering me. Baba then went back inside his room.

From this moment, I knew with certainty and from the depths of my soul that not only was Baba my Guru, but that I was also his disciple.

Following this retreat, was one last satsang at the Universalist Church on Seventy-sixth Street and Central Park West in Manhattan. On the stage with Baba Muktananda was Swami Satchidananda, Baba Ram Dass, and I believe, Pir Vilayat Khan. That morning Baba had given me a shaker instrument and asked me to take it to the evening satsang, which I did. I played it during the chant that evening. The chanting was sublime.

7. ON THE WAY TO INDIA

A few weeks after Baba left New York to continue his First World Tour to Texas, California, and Hawaii, I was finally ready to set off for India. I was traveling with Ann and Arnie Harris, a married couple I had met at Big Indian. They were both hatha yoga instructors in New York. At that time there were student fares on many airlines. We were able to get a flight for ninety dollars from New York to London, and we expected to be able to get another ninety-dollar flight from London to Bombay (now Mumbai).

When we got to London, however, we found that those low fares were no longer available. We spent five days in London trying to find an inexpensive flight. I didn't really have the funds for a pricier ticket, and besides, I was planning for only a one-way trip. Finally, with some assistance from my travel mates, we booked a flight on Egypt Air. A few hours after take-off, the pilot announced that we were going to make an unscheduled stop in Cairo to pick up some passengers. When we landed, we were informed that the new passengers had been delayed and couldn't get to us until the next day. We were taken to a nearby hotel for the night. As we walked through the airport as a group, there were airport workers who seemed excited to see us. One man, with great enthusiasm, handed me a tiny picture of Gamal Abdel Nasser, the former president of Egypt, as he said in broken English, "Yes, we love him."

It was now about 10:00 p.m. On the bus ride to the hotel, we saw that there were people thronging the streets. A holiday celebration of some sort was going on. There were food stands lit up with lights, music blaring, and camels walking in the crowded streets. It was the first time I had ever been in a culture that was dramatically different from my own. I was experiencing a bit of culture shock, and I felt a little uneasy. It all seemed unreal.

When we arrived at the hotel, my first question was, "How far away are we from the Great Sphinx and the pyramids?" We were told this was all about a half hour away by taxi. We didn't have to be at the airport until later that morning, so we arranged for a taxi to pick us up at 5:30 a.m. to take us to see these ancient monuments. We arrived soon after sunrise, and there were no other tourists around. I will never forget standing between the outstretched arms of the sphinx, looking up at his massive head from underneath it.

That morning, the sunrise was a brilliant gold and red, and there was a cloud passing just overhead. It was a timeless moment that marked my entrance to the East.

*   *   *

Finally, we arrived in Bombay. Arnie and Ann had some interest in traveling in India a bit before going on to Ganeshpuri. We knew that Baba Muktananda wouldn't actually be there for another month. They had heard stories about Sathya Sai Baba in Puttaparthi, which is near Bangalore in the south. I didn't really have interest in going there, but as we were traveling companions, I went along. We took a train to Bangalore and then a bus to Puttaparthi.

It was evening by the time we arrived. We were not expected but were given a room to share. Early the next morning, a man knocked on our door and said that Sai Baba wanted to see us and that we were to come with him. We were taken to a small room with a large chair and were directed to sit on the floor. (By this time, I knew enough not to sit in the big chair!)

Sai Baba came in and instead of sitting on the chair, he sat on the floor with us. He was well known for making things appear in his hands, like holy ash, which he would sprinkle on people as he walked through a crowd. Sometimes he would seemingly manifest trinkets that he would give as gifts.

He was very gracious to us and spoke to each of us individually. When he spoke to Ann, he swung his index finger around in front of him and a pearl necklace appeared, which he gave to her. I was sitting not five feet from him and took note that I couldn't see any sleight of hand. Ann seemed to be quite taken by him. That evening she said she didn't need to go any further and was going to stay there in Puttaparthi. Arnie agreed, and that was that.

I felt that I needed to continue on to Ganeshpuri to be with Baba, so I left after a few days. Before leaving, I met an American man named Jaidevi, who had also spent time with Hilda Charlton in New York. Jaidevi was staying in Bangalore with a yogi named Shiva Bala Yogi and insisted that I meet him.

Shiva Bala Yogi's story, which I read in a pamphlet, was remarkable. When he was fourteen, while playing with some friends, he opened a palmyra fruit from which he heard the unmistakable sound of *Om*. He then saw a bright light in his hands. The form of a yogi who was smeared with ash and dressed like Lord Shiva appeared and told Shiva Bali Yogi to sit down, close his eyes, and meditate. Apparently, he did so—twenty-three hours a day for the next twelve years. His mother took care of him during this time. I saw a number of photographs of this yogi, taken over the course of those twelve years. They were quite extraordinary and, being only twenty-one myself at the time, I was inspired by them. I still have copies of those photos in my computer.

Nevertheless, I knew that I had to continue on. I had to be with my Baba. I took a train from Bangalore to Bombay and then caught a bus to Ganeshpuri. While on the train, I realized that I was beginning to feel uneasy and disoriented. I think I was still experiencing a bit of culture shock. Then at one point the train stopped at a station to pick up passengers, and I looked out the window and saw a *sadhu*, an Indian holy man, standing beside the train. He looked directly at me, silently folded his palms in *namaskar*, and his gaze seemed to dissolve all my anxiety. I knew I was on the right path. The rest of the trip was very peaceful.

8. Arriving in Ganeshpuri

I hadn't given any notice that I was arriving, but when I entered Shree Gurudev Ashram, I was taken right away into a small courtyard near the dining room where Baba Muktananda was sitting. At the time this was the main courtyard where he gave daily *darshan*. It served adequately for the thirty-five or so Westerners and about that number of Indians who were the residents of the ashram at that time.

Baba had arrived from his first world tour just four days earlier, He was sitting in the courtyard with only one other person, Mr. Raisada, an Indian gentleman who, as it happened, spoke perfect English.

Baba smiled and called me over. He pulled me onto his lap, hugging me and rubbing my head over and over, saying, "Ah, you have come."

He then raised two fingers with his palm facing up and waved his fingers questioningly. I knew exactly what he meant as Mr. Raisada asked, "There were two others?"

I knew he meant Ann and Arnie. I told Baba that they had remained in the South, and he pulled me onto his lap again, rubbing my head and saying, "*Bahut accha, bahut accha*"—"very good, very good." I knew he was referring to the fact that, even though my friends had chosen to stay behind, I was determined to be with him. I could feel that Baba was pleased. I must have had a smile on my face from ear to ear. I felt my long journey was finally complete. I was right where I needed to be. I was home.

*   *   *

It is hard to describe the following weeks and months in Baba's ashram. Although we were a small group during the week, hundreds would arrive every weekend from Bombay and other nearby towns to spend a few days with their guru. Some people traveled hours to do this. On festival days, many thousands would come. Even with all that fluctuation, there was a steadiness about life in the ashram. I thrived on the fixed schedule and discipline of the daily routines. It was just what I needed.

We woke to loud gongs from the main temple at 3:30 a.m. In those days the bathhouse was located a short walk away, in the lower gardens. There was a large tank of water that was heated each morning. A Dutch boy named Robbie would light the fire at 1:00 a.m. so the water would be hot by 3:30. We would draw some hot water into a plastic bucket, and then, in the bathing area, bathe from the bucket using a cup.

An hour of meditation followed, and then we could go to the dining room for chai. After this we recited a sacred text in the main temple. Baba was always there for the recitation, and he taught us, sometimes sternly, how to pace the phrasing of the texts. He would tap out the cadence with a little stick he called his *chota guruji* his "little guru." If you fell asleep, it would not be unusual for him to throw something at you. It could be anything. One day an Australian boy who worked in the woodshop made a wooden rack of one-inch squares. Each of these had rounded edges and was engraved with an *Om* sign. When this was presented to Baba, he got quite a laugh as it was explained to him that they were for throwing at sleeping yogis. He played with them, but I don't recall him actually tossing one at anyone.

In those days the morning recitation was chapters of *Shri Bhagavad Gita*, followed by two *namasankirtanas*—two traditional call-and-response chants. These were ecstatic and ended soon after sunrise. Regardless of what chapter of *Shri Bhagavad Gita* we were up to on Friday, when the weekend came—the time when there were many people coming from Bombay—we would always recite chapter 13, "The Field and the Knower of the Field." Here, the Self is described as "the knower of the field," and the world itself is seen as a field in which we reap whatever we have sown. Baba seemed to want to press the point that we must not reject the world but must take responsibility for our relationship with the world.

Baba always had me sit with the main group of men that sat very close to him. We all chanted with great enthusiasm. What a way to start the day! The golden glow of the sunrise through the front gate of the ashram, plus the elevated mood of the chants, left me feeling very full as I exited the hall each day. My whole being was energized. Birds were singing their morning songs. The smell of the earth blending with incense was nourishing. The deepest part of me was fulfilled in the beauty of those mornings.

This was followed by a few hours of *seva*, selfless service, in the ashram. We all had our respective tasks, which could change at any time. My first task was to sweep and clean the hallways and guest rooms in Turiya Mandir, a building in the upper garden that was used by special guests. It also contained a large and beautiful meditation room. Swami Prakashananda, one of Baba's earliest disciples, always stayed there when he visited. Baba Ram Dass stayed there. The Karmapa, the sixteenth in his line, stayed there. . . It was an honor for me to meet these guests and to serve them.

There was one permanent resident in Turiya Mandir, and that was Babu Shetty, an old disciple of Bhagavan Nityananda. Babu Shetty had met Bhagavan Nityananda when Babu was just a child. He had visited Bhagavan throughout his life. After Babu retired and moved to Ganeshpuri, Bhagavan instructed Baba Muktananda to take care of him. Babu Shetty and I shared many stories.

Every day, I swept the floors with the bundled dried coconut fronds that were used as brooms. Every day, I would come across an army of ants marching across the floor. I was always horrified that I was killing, or at least disturbing, these blessed creatures. One day, I asked Baba about this. "Am I creating bad karma by killing ants in this sacred space?" Baba laughed and said "Don't worry, your job is to remove the ants. You'll send them on to a better life." I was reminded of the section of the *Bhagavad Gita* where Krishna is instructing Arjuna, who was reluctant to engage in battle, that his duty was to fight. Well, I certainly sent many an ant along to a better existence after that. I did it, however, with reverence.

Following morning seva, at eleven o'clock we would all gather in the main hall where Professor Jain would read to Baba the letters from devotees around the world, and Baba would respond. After this, we could ask any questions we might have about spirituality or *sadhana*, the spiritual path. These precious conversations were collected and published in his books *Satsang with Baba*, volumes 1 through 5, and in another of Baba's books of questions and answers, *Paramartha Katha Prasang*, which was compiled by Amma. We were so fortunate to have that time with Baba each day.

After lunch, we would rest or go to the temple to chant. At that time, we were reciting *Shri Guru Gita* after lunch. In later years the schedule changed, and we did the recitation of *Shri Guru Gita* in the morning and the *Vishnu Sahasranam* after lunch. Following the lunch period and the after-lunch recitation, was another period of seva. After seva, Baba would sit in the courtyard where we could be with him again for a while. In those days during the public darshans we all stood the entire time, even if it went on for hours. Sitting for darshan didn't begin until we returned after Baba's second world tour in 1976. I remember some of the Indian devotees being surprised that we would now sit in our guru's presence. Baba had to tell them many times to sit. This was followed by the evening *Arati* chant and a light dinner. After dinner, we would recite the *Shiva Mahimna Stotram* in the temple and then retire early around 8:30 or 9:00 p.m.

*　　　*　　　*

I used to chant wholeheartedly. Chanting was something I could do that would always elevate my state, regardless of whatever else was going on. At that point in my life, I was trying hard to regain the state I had initially experienced spontaneously—and had touched again in my early experiences with Baba. I wanted nothing else. I think I may have been trying to "crash the gates of heaven." I still had a lot to learn. At quiet times in the ashram, I would stand silently next to Baba's seat in the courtyard and try to feel his presence. I didn't make many friends in the ashram—but, then I wasn't interested in anything but Baba. All I wanted was God, and Baba was my doorway to that experience.

Looking back, I understand why some people thought I was too intense. I was just twenty-one—six or seven years younger than most of the other Westerners in the ashram. Many had been professors or had held accomplished positions. Many struggled with the overall discipline of the ashram. However, I threw myself into it with all that I had, and I loved it. I think there were people who resented me for this.

When I chanted, I was trying to reach God. I was totally consumed and focused. Fortunately, I have a decent singing voice. Baba seemed to like it anyway, as he always had me sit right in front of him. Once when Baba was out of the ashram for a few weeks, Venkappa Shriyan, an ashram manager who was very stern with the Western men in those days, would pull me out of the hall and make me chant outside. When Baba returned, he brought me back in and sat me right in front of him again.

My first room in the ashram was in the upper garden—a thatched hut with a cow-dung floor. This hut had been used as a cow shed until a new cow shed was built at the back of the upper gardens. After a week or so, I was offered a room that was under the steps of one of the guest cottages. This new room was about six feet long and four feet wide. It had a slanted ceiling as it was below the steps. These days it's used as a closet for gardening tools. I was very happy with this room as it was private and gave me a place where I could meditate in peace. I was able to stretch out and lay down fully for sleep and when sitting for meditation I could sit in a lotus position with about two inches on either side of my knees.

One day while meditating there, I fell into a state that Baba calls *tandra*. It is a state in which you are neither awake nor asleep. In this meditation, I found myself in the hall of a being who was sitting on a golden throne that was in the shape of a bull. This being had skin that was pitch black in color. Not a dark African brown but black as black can be—like black lacquer. His eyes were wide open and bright. He wore a red *dhoti* from his waist down and was bare chested. He may have worn the traditional Brahmin thread. He leaned forward, bending toward me with his hands on his knees and was smiling at me benevolently. I had no idea who he was, but I felt he was giving me a blessing. I had never had an experience like this before, and I never told Baba about it. Some years later, I read a description of Lord Yama, the god of death, that was exactly like this. The memory of the experience still fills me with wonder.

During this time, in the ashram we had no books in English other than a small book, *Ashram Dharma*, which laid out all the rules and expectations of ashram living. Baba's spiritual autobiography, *Chitshakti Vilas*, had not yet been published in English. There were two English translations that were being circulated among ashramites. These were in blue folders on legal-sized onion-skin paper. Once you got the folder, you could keep it for a week. I remember passing it forward after only a few days, having read only a few pages. I was having so many new experiences and changes that I couldn't quite digest it.

The first official English edition was published by Harper and Rowe in late 1971 under the name *Guru*. It was only the first part of the book—Baba's own story and not his advice on sadhana—as the publisher wanted to see how the book sold before publishing a second edition with everything in it. Baba didn't really want that. After changing publishers, the second edition was renamed to its original title, *Chitshakti Vilas*, and included the full manuscript. Later English editions translated the title to *The Play of Consciousness*. For Siddha Yogis, it's a foundational text.

*   *   *

One day following lunch, I decided to meditate outside my room in the sun. This felt very natural to me after I'd spent so much time in Hawaii. I meditated peacefully for a half hour or so. The next morning, I woke up with my whole face very swollen. My eyes were almost swollen shut. It was a bit painful as well.

I came down for the morning chant and was taken to Gopal Desai, another ashram manager, who took me right to Baba. I was told to wait in the temple. Baba came out and gave me an amla fruit that was preserved in syrup. He told me to go outside the temple, eat it, and then come in for the chant. He said he would bring this to me every morning for three days. He also admonished me saying, "In India you can't sunbathe. The sun here is poison." As soon as the fruit touched my tongue, all the pain disappeared.

The next day, Baba brought an amla fruit to me again with the same instructions to go outside the temple, eat the fruit, and come in for the chant. On the third day, Baba came without the fruit. That was fine with me. The pain was already gone, and I was not disappointed that he never brought the third amla fruit. I did get a nice smile in its place.

The climate in India can be quite severe. I have often said there are three seasons in India. One is too hot; one is too wet; and one is too cold. The hot season, which runs from about mid-March until early June, can be tortuous. The temperatures can easily be 110 degrees Fahrenheit during the day, and it never really cools down much at night. My brain felt like the mirages of water that you see on a road in the distance on a very hot day. It seemed that everyone was talking about when the expected monsoon rains would finally come to cool things down. It was hard to eat or even think during the hot season.

India is almost completely dependent on its monsoon rains. Typically, there is no rain for the rest of the year. Everything dries up. The ground becomes cracked and barren. I remember one monsoon when we were all anxiously waiting for the rains to begin. Looking east from the front gate, we began to see dark clouds appearing off on the horizon. Then cooling winds came, followed by heavy rain.

I was watching this as a group of young boys, maybe eight or ten years old, gathered in a dirt area just across the street from the front gate of the ashram. They had a one-man plow and began taking turns running in circles with it. This went on for about twenty minutes. I couldn't figure out what they were doing. It became clear when the rain finally arrived. The rain quickly filled the hole they had just made and turned it into an instant swimming hole. They tossed aside the plow, and all gleefully jumped in, laughing and squealing and shouting with jubilation. They knew exactly what was coming and what to do about it.

One year the monsoon never arrived. Apparently, it had changed course and rained over the ocean for three months leaving India very dry. There is a lot of rice grown throughout India. No monsoon meant no rice, which is India's staple food. During this time, we ate more chapattis, flat breads made of wheat, at meals instead of rice. Wheat could still be grown in the north. We may have had rice once a week. Any rice grown was collected by the government and redistributed throughout the region. There was no Amrit snack shop at that time to supplement our Western tastes. There was only a small tea shop next door run by a man named Sena. He mostly sold chai and some small snacks. You could order a lunch meal the day before if you wanted. I rarely frequented the shop as my funds were minimal.

During this dry year, the ashram wells became very low, and we were restricted to one fourth of a bucket of water per day for our morning bath and to wash our clothes. We learned the technique of standing on a piece of clothing, then pouring water with a cup over our head, body, and clothing, followed by gentle soaping and rinsing. If you managed this carefully, you could clean one piece of clothing per day.

There were other hardships as well, which I should say I bore willingly. They were all worth the dynamic experiences I was having. For example, in these early days there was no breakfast served, only a large lunch and a light dinner. As this was hard on the Westerners, chapattis and chai began to be served after the morning chant for the Westerners. We would be given two chapatis each. If you wanted more, you had to ask Baba personally for permission. Once a week there might be some special addition like *kitchari*, which is a blend of yellow lentils, rice, and some spices. We always looked forward to this.

There was no medical assistance at that time either. There was a small cabinet near the office that had some bandages, a bottle of aspirin, and a few odd things that people left behind when they went home.

So, it was hard. You really had to want to be there. However, Baba's presence was everywhere, and this was so powerful that it overrode all the hardships. In his presence there was so much spiritual energy flowing that it was unmistakable. Like coming before a fire, you couldn't help but feel the heat. Coming anywhere near Baba, you couldn't help but feel uplifted and energized.

Baba was the embodiment of everything I was looking for. He seemed like a lion. He was so strong, yet so compassionate. He could be like a mother, a father, a grandfather, or a grandmother. He could be my captain or my king. I felt I was living in the court of God.

9. SMALL MIRACLES EVERY DAY

Baba was awakening such powerful energy in everyone. This is so rare. *Shaktipat*, or the awakening of Kundalini by a Siddha Master, traditionally was given only after a long period of preparation involving study and service to the Guru. Baba gave this awakening freely and to everyone. It sometimes felt like an explosion in my being that was dramatically transforming me from within. Everyone in the ashram seemed to be having similar experiences. We always looked forward to seeing new people arrive. It was fun to watch their transformation and hear their stories as they adapted to the energy of the ashram.

For a while the seva I offered was in the cowshed, feeding the cows and minding them in the fields. One day the whole herd of sixteen cows was being led to a grazing pasture off to the side of the cowshed. The cows were almost at the gate when Baba appeared from the opposite direction. As if on signal, at the sound of his voice, every cow simultaneously turned her head in his direction and then, with a seemingly joyful gait, went over to him. Baba stood there talking lovingly to each animal and was petting them all. I've never seen a herd of cows respond in quite that way to anyone. But then Baba was far from being just anyone.

At one point, I was among a group of men who moved our rooms to the cowshed in the upper gardens. I loved walking back to the cowshed across the fields at night after the evening chant. The air was so fresh and sweet. The sky was so clear and the stars so bright. It was the first time that I could see the Southern Cross constellation, which is only visible that far south. There was always the accompaniment of the night birds that filled the air with a whirly kind of sound.

Living in the back of the ashram meant that we couldn't access the main meditation room or the temple until 4:00 a.m., when the gate to the lower gardens was opened. By 4:30, there were chants being played over the loudspeaker system. These were beautiful, but they interfered with the silence that I wanted in order to meditate peacefully. This prompted me to start getting up at 2:00 a.m. so I could finish meditating before the chants came on.

I would get up and take a cold-water bath under a nearby water spigot and then sit for a while near the large well that was just outside the cowshed. Early one morning, I was standing next to the well when I was surprised to see the figure of a woman who seemed to float off of the top of the mountain above the nearby Vajreshwari Temple. She was silvery white, transparent, and luminous. She floated across the fields and then disappeared into the well. I felt there was some connection between the Vajreshwari Temple and that well. I thought of her as the Lady of the Well. I never told Baba about this experience, but years later Baba told a story about once having had a vision of the Vajreshwari Devi in that same form I had seen. Baba said that in this vision, the goddess had instructed him to build that well.

As the weather got colder, I started looking for a warm spot to meditate. The well had a small pump house next to it with a few steps leading down into it. I thought this looked like a quiet space, so for a few nights I went down there to meditate. One afternoon, I happened to look around and was a bit shocked to see a black snake wound around a pipe. I don't know if the snake was actually there when I was, but I definitely changed my chosen spot for meditation.

*   *   *

One day as I was working in the upper garden, someone came to tell me that Baba wanted to see me right away. I found Baba sitting in the small courtyard near the dining hall. Only Venkappa and Ram

Chadha, an Indian engineer, were there with him. Baba said something very sweet directed to me. Venkappa immediately responded and what sounded like a strong conversation ensued between them. I had no idea what was going on. They spoke in Marathi, and nothing was being translated for me. After a few minutes of this, Baba stood up and went back inside, and Venkappa abruptly left the courtyard. I asked Mr. Chadha, who spoke perfect English, what this was all about. At first, he wouldn't tell me, saying, "It's OK, it's OK." I said, "It's not OK. Obviously, it was about me. What did Baba say?"

Mr. Chadha then told me that Baba had wanted me to take his car and drive it to Delhi, where he would later meet me as he was going out on tour. I would then drive Baba for the rest of the tour. Venkappa had objected strongly, saying that I didn't know how to drive in India and that I shouldn't do it. He felt an Indian driver should be selected. Baba apparently gave in to this eventually, and that was that.

I let it go. I remembered how Baba had told me back in New York that I would drive him and that we would travel together all over India. While it's true that I had never driven in the very busy and seemingly no-rules-of-the-road India, I did feel that I was an experienced driver and would likely have been able to learn the skills easily enough. In later years, Venkappa and I became good friends. He had been the first permanent resident of the ashram, and he was always devoted to Baba. I have a lot of respect for him.

Baba did go on tour for almost two months at that time. I stayed back in the ashram and continued the daily routines. I was meditating very well just by sitting quietly and remembering Baba, but at some point, I began to reflect that I had never asked for or received a mantra from him. It was most common that this was the first step when people wanted to engage with Baba. He would typically hand them a mantra card, which was printed with a message from him and the *Om Namah Shivaya* mantra. Occasionally, Baba would tell someone to repeat *Guru Om*. I began to think perhaps I was missing something. I felt that since Baba was away, I would choose one of these two mantras and begin using it.

After mentally trying out both mantras, I felt that *Guru Om* was more comfortable and easier to pace with my breathing. For the next month, I began to experience a real sweetness with this practice. I was sure that Baba would tell me to use the *Guru Om* mantra.

A few days after Baba's return, I approached him at a morning question and answer session. I explained my dilemma regarding my choice of mantra and said that I wanted clarity. Professor Jain was translating. I knew enough Hindi to know that Jain simply said, "He wants a mantra." Baba then handed me a mantra card. I tried to explain that there was more to it, but I couldn't get Jain's attention. Feeling frustrated, I finally went back to my seat. I was a bit upset about this.

Over the next few days, I tried to use the *Om Namah Shivaya* mantra, but it felt too long. One morning, after seva, I had the strong urge to go into the village of Ganeshpuri to the shrine of Baba's guru, Bhagavan Nityananda. I offered a coconut there and prayed for help in my practice. As I was leaving, the temple priest gave me an orange as *prasad*. While walking back to our ashram, I was reciting *Om Namah Shivaya*, synchronizing the mantra with each step. My mind began to become more and more focused, and then suddenly, like a feather being lifted into a gentle breeze, I was carried into a state of rapture. The sound of *Om Namah Shivaya* was pulsating in every pore of my body. All I could think, all I could feel, all I could see was *Om Namah Shivaya Om Namah Shivaya*. Visually, the entire world around me seemed to be made up of the mantra. Each individual object, every leaf of every tree, their branches, a cloud, a stone, the road. . . each one seemed to spell out *Om Namah Shivaya* millions of times. It was if an artist had drawn a picture using only the words *Om Namah Shivaya* to create all the forms. The entire universe was filled with the mantra, and this seemed to be its natural state. Everything praised Shiva, the Divine, the eternal Self of all.

As I slowly came down from this state, I marveled at how it was that when all of nature, including the very stones on the ground, seemed to exist in a natural state of worship of the supreme, how could it be that man has to struggle so much to recognize it.

Needless to say, from this experience, I clearly understood that it was certainly OK to repeat *Om Namah Shivaya* as my mantra. When I reached the ashram, Baba was sitting out. He looked at me with a knowing smile. The mantra has been with me since that day.

*   *   *

Things went on like this for some time. Stories and miracles every day it seemed. Although I immersed myself in the ashram routines all I really wanted to do was to meditate. Early on I remember being led up to the upper garden and being asked to clean out a shallow pit that surrounded a coconut tree. After a while, Gopal Desai, the ashram manager, came by and told me to fill the pit back in. He said, "So you want to learn to meditate? Then work hard." I didn't quite understand at the time, but this became central to the pattern of my spiritual journey. I wanted only to meditate; I wanted peace and quiet to be able to meditate, but that was not Baba's real message. He wanted more for us than just meditation. He wanted his students to be able to integrate the state of meditation into our daily lives. Baba was fond of saying that a person, without leaving their job, without leaving their family, could meditate and realize the Truth within their own being. It seemed that every time I wanted to focus only on meditation, I would be thrown into a situation where I had to engage even more. This became a central theme for me throughout all the years of my sadhana. I still had a lot to assimilate. I had to learn this lesson again and again.

I had received a very intense *shaktipat*, a spiritual awakening, from Baba. There were courses of energy moving through my body all throughout the day, even when I was not meditating. All I wanted to do was to absorb myself in this. I became very thin, even emaciated. I had a voracious appetite. Even after eating, I would sit down and this shakti energy would rise up and consume me. I went down to 104 pounds. I'm currently five-foot-seven, and I weigh 163, so what I underwent at that time was a tremendous weight loss. Baba even had me checked out by a visiting medical doctor, a well-known cardiologist, who took me on his rounds and then to a hospital in Bombay, where I was examined and spent two nights. My roommate that night was a young Jain monk. The Jains are very particular and focus on absolute nonviolence. This monk was plucking his beard the next morning and told me that it was good to occasionally feel pain. The experience of being there was interesting. The nurses didn't understand why I was there, especially as I had a good appetite and kept asking for more of the biscuits that were being served with chai. I was found to be in excellent health, and I came back to the ashram the next day.

In one of Baba's writings, he explained that becoming emaciated can happen after a strong shaktipat awakening as the shakti consumes impurities from the body. There were a few other ashramites who had a similar experience.

*   *   *

Shree Gurudev Ashram—Baba changed the ashram's name to Gurudev Siddha Peeth in 1978—was built around three original rooms that Bhagavan Nityananda had built for Baba in the mid-1950s and where he had instructed Baba to stay. This is now the site of Baba's *Samadhi Shrine*. In the early days there was a small room, perhaps six by six feet, that Baba used for meditation. Later, he would sometimes send a special guest to meditate there, and many described extraordinary experiences. Surrounding that room were four corridors with cushions all around for ashramites to meditate. An entrance to Baba's quarters was there as well. There were also steps that led down to an underground room we called the Cave. The Cave was underneath Baba's rooms and a very powerful place for meditation. We sometimes had twenty-four-hour long chants of the *Om Namah Shivaya* mantra there. Baba would join us for hours at a time. Above the Cave, the original walls of Baba's meditation room were eventually removed at Baba's request some months prior to his *mahasamadhi* in 1982. Clearly, he had anticipated his final passing. He now resides in the exact place his Guru told him to stay.

My favorite spot to sit was against the wall in the east corridor, where the entranceway to his Samadhi Shrine now exists, as the walls have since been removed. Sometimes soon after I sat down, I would be energized so strongly that I couldn't move. It felt like I was being electrocuted with a thousand volts of electricity. It was so powerful. I would hear popping sounds in my head as these sensations that were like electricity grew stronger. It felt as if nerve pathways were being opened and that I was being rewired. This would happen several times a week. I knew it was a beneficial experience as it always left me in a wonderfully energized state.

One morning while I was meditating, I went into a *tandra* state, neither awake nor asleep. I saw my mother as a young girl blissfully walking in the woods. There was a strong energy present. Many years later when I was talking with my mother, she told me a story that she said she had never shared with anyone before. When she was about sixteen years old and was hiking with my father in a wooded area, she suddenly melted into the forest and couldn't distinguish herself from the beauty surrounding her. My mother said that throughout her life, during difficult times, she would often remember that experience, and it always brought her peace.

When she told me her story, I remembered my earlier experience of seeing her in my meditation and the peace that surrounded her. Baba once said that when a disciple receives shaktipat from the guru, this initiation affects seven generations behind and seven generations forward. How flexible is time and space? Is it possible that a blessing like this can transcend time and space?

*   *   *

Soon the men's dormitory was finished on the second floor of the main building, and I moved into it. This building was a greatly expanded structure. There were now four floors. The Sadhu Dorm, as it was called, was just above the main Temple and housed about twenty men. At that time, we all had mattresses on the floor and a small cubby for our belongings. Later, simple beds were added. The Temple itself was being expanded. The statue of Bhagavan Nityananda hadn't been installed there yet. Against the south wall was a life-sized photograph of Baba's Guru, and this was the focal point of the Temple. Baba's chair was on the west wall. Bhagavan Nityananda's statue was installed in May of 1971.

Around this time, I had a conversation with one of the men living in the ashram in which it became evident that I actually knew his father, Herb Kruckman, and had for many years. He had been a regular visitor to the summer camp I used to attend in New York. Herb Kruckman was an artist with an engaging skill. He would ask one of the campers to join him at the front of the room and to make any kind of arbitrary line or squiggle on a large drawing tablet. Mr. Kruckman would then proceed to make up a story and to enlarge on this one line to form a picture of the story he was telling. His main character was always a boy named Yonkel Bonkel. That was what we called Mr. Kruckman: Yonkel Bonkel. His son and I had a good laugh as he learned that having come all this way to India, I knew Yonkel Bonkel.

I became friends with a young man visiting from then-communist East Germany. He was a student of philosophy there. It had taken him nine years to get a visa so that he could study Eastern philosophy in India. Once his long-awaited visa was approved, he quickly arranged to visit India. While in Bombay, he heard about Baba's ashram and came to visit. He had wonderful meditation experiences, and he was quite taken with Baba. I was present at the end of his stay as he made his arrangements to go back home.

He asked Baba, "How can I teach meditation to my countrymen when teaching religion isn't permitted there?"

Baba laughed and said, "Tell them you learned a new way to sleep." He then added, "Don't worry, in twenty-five years there will be no communism in your country. However, it will arise in other places."

This was 1971. The Berlin Wall fell in 1989. It just so happened that before this young man from East Germany left the ashram, the first German translation of *Chitshakti Vilas* was published and was available in the ashram bookstore. I purchased a copy and gave it to him as a going away present.

Later, in 1975, while in Oakland, California, a young Romanian woman approached Baba and essentially asked the same question. Baba told her not to worry because in twenty years there would be no communism in her country. I took note that it had been about five years since he'd said that in twenty-five years communism would end in East Germany.

And so, it continued like this. Days, weeks and months, miracles, and stories daily. Late one night in the men's dorm, I heard a loud yell from the lower garden. "Baba! Baba! Baba!" someone called. I ran to see what was happening. Baba was already there. An Italian woman, Chitralekha, had just stepped on and been stung by a scorpion. Baba took her hand and raised it high, yelling, "Guru Om!" Her pain seemed to stop immediately. Baba laughed and said, "Don't worry. You might feel a bit numb in your foot tomorrow morning, but you will be OK."

Amma, a Sanskrit scholar who had been Baba's secretary for many years, once related a story to me that she personally witnessed. This occurred on a celebration day some years before. On holidays like that, the ashram would feed a few thousand people for lunch. Devotees would arrive from all over India. Baba would also distribute cloth and utensils to the local villagers. Toward the end of the feast that day, Baba was told that a whole busload of people who had been delayed on the road would be arriving soon. The problem was that there was no more rice, as it had all been distributed to the crowds that had arrived earlier.

Baba instructed the kitchen to place a cloth over the large serving tray that was typically used for rice and to just serve the food from under the cloth. Baba told them not to lift the cloth, just keep serving. They did this, and the rice kept coming. The servers were amazed, but they followed Baba's instructions to the letter. Just as the last person was served, the rice ran out.

Even though things like this did happen around Baba, the real miracles were the transformations in the lives of the people who came to him. And this was something very inspiring to witness.

10. Shirdi

After some months had passed, I began to feel a bit restless. I confided in Professor Jain, who took me to Baba. I told Baba that I loved being there but shared my feeling of restlessness. He looked at me and said I should go to Shirdi for ten days. Shirdi is one of the holiest sites in India, visited by people of all faiths. It was four or five hours away by bus yet still in Maharashtra. It had been the home of Sai Baba of Shirdi, and it now housed his samadhi shrine. Sai Baba had lived from 1838 to 1918, and he is considered one of the greatest saints of India.

On the way to Shirdi, I made a side trip to Alandi, to the tomb of the thirteenth-century Maharashtrian saint, Jnaneshwar Maharaj. Baba spoke of him often. It is said that Jnaneshwar took live samadhi—that is, he entered his tomb alive, went into deep meditation, and still remains in the tomb, in meditation and as alive as he ever was. While in Alandi, I was invited to visit a school for young boys, who were being trained to play the *kartals*, a sweet cymbal instrument. I met a man there who invited me to stay in his small hotel. When I got there, he told me he was a poet and had written many poems. He asked if I would like to hear some and proceeded to recite and sing many beautiful devotional poems of Alandi, Jnaneshwar, and the lovely surrounding area. This man went on with his recitations for about two hours with great feeling and enthusiasm. Following this, I had a good night's rest and then traveled on.

*　　　*　　　*

I arrived in Shirdi the next day and first went to Sai Baba's samadhi shrine. A life-sized white marble statue of him had been installed on top of his tomb. In life, Sai Baba had been neither Muslim nor Hindu. He respected all and people of all faiths came to see him. There were beautiful aratis sung several times a day in the shrine, and I went to most of these. To keep up with my practices I meditated regularly and chanted *Shri Guru Gita* three times a day. I slept on the grounds in a garden, known as the Lendi Bhag. There was a platform there with an oil lamp that was kept lit. I later learned that Sai Baba had been fond of this spot and would often sit there. I also frequently visited a small hut known as Dwarkamai, where Sai Baba would sleep and sit during the day. He tended a fire in this hut, and he would distribute ash from the fire to devotees as blessings and medicine for their ailments. This fire has been maintained to this day.

I befriended a *sadhu* who was then the caretaker of Dwarkamai, and we had many beautiful conversations. I still have some ash from this fire. Sometimes if a devotee was in need, Sai Baba would reach into his coat pocket and pull out a few coins. He was known to have said, "I give them what they want in the hope that they will begin to want what I want to give them."

One day in the Lendi Bhag, I met a young Indian seeker who insisted that I needed to meet someone. This young man took me to the back of the village of Shirdi to a small hut. We went in, and he introduced me to Marthand Maharaj, a very elderly man who was the son of Mhalsapati, the man who had first greeted Sai Baba in Shirdi in the 1850s. This man, Mhalsapati, had been the caretaker of a small village temple and had found the young holy man in the nearby forest. Mhalsapati had greeted the holy man and invited him into the town, saying, *"Ao Sai,"* meaning "Come Lord." This is how Sai Baba received the name he was known by. Mhalsapati became one of Sai Baba's closest disciples. I have a photo of Mhalsapati with Sai Baba, showing a very young Marthand resting his head in Sai Baba's lap.

After we sat down in the room, Marthand Maharaj looked at me and said with great enthusiasm, "You have been here before."

I politely said, no, and that this was my first trip to India.

Mhalsapati then raised his hand high as he said, "By the power of Sai, you have been here before!"

I felt he must have been picking up on the energy of my meditations, so this time, I just smiled and said nothing.

Marthand Maharaj then proceeded to open a cabinet and take out Sai Baba's coat and cane, placing both in my lap. This was the same coat from which Sai Baba used to pull coins to give to people in need. I was quite amazed—and honored—that I was sitting there with these sacred objects that had belonged to this great being.

The next few days passed with great beauty, but, still, I was anxious to get back to Ganeshpuri.

*   *   *

Ten days after I'd left Shirdi Sai Baba's ashram, I began my journey back to Ganeshpuri. I hadn't announced my arrival time to anyone, but when my bus stopped in front of the ashram, Professor Jain was walking out of the front gate. He told me that Baba had sent him to tell me that I should stay in the village of Ganeshpuri for a while. I felt he saw that I was having a positive experience, and he wanted me to have more time by myself to relish and assimilate it

The village of Ganeshpuri is about three quarters of a mile down the road from Shree Gurudev Ashram. I walked there and went first to Bhagavan Nityananda's samadhi shrine, paid my respects, and sat quietly for a while. In the evenings I slept behind the shrine, where there is a small Krishna temple. I slept between the *murti* of Lord Krishna and the samadhi shrine. Sometimes I slept in a hallway that was just outside the hall where Bhagavan used to hold darshan. I slept on the ground. All I had with me was a blanket and a small burlap satchel of things I carried which would also be my pillow. During the day, I went back to Baba's ashram and spent the day in the main temple. I attended all the ashram chants, and I began to copy the words to the *Arati* and *Shri Guru Gita* in a small notebook for my future reference. At that time there were no printed English copies of *Shri Guru Gita* other than a few mimeographed versions in a pink construction-paper cover.

This was the time that the new murti of Bhagavan Nityananda was being installed in the main hall at Shree Gurudev Ashram. Celebrations were ramping up. Baba now allowed me to have my meals in the ashram. To save time walking back and forth from the village, I began to sleep in the open field that was in front of the ashram. I participated in all the ashram festivities. Soon, I was able to rejoin the normal ashram routines, and I was back in the Sadhu Dorm.

About this time, I began to wonder about going back to America to find a quiet place, maybe on a simple farm, so that I could focus on meditation. I felt I needed to absorb everything that had been happening to me. I guess I still didn't understand the extent to which I had to assimilate my inner experience with my outer life. I spoke to Baba about this.

Baba's response was, "Yes, it would be good for you to go back to America now. You should go to New York City and drive a taxicab. Also go to school and take some classes."

This was far from what I'd had in mind—far from what I'd expected! But I was willing to follow his instructions.

11. OVERLAND JOURNEY, 1971

I made my plans to return to the States. I didn't have much money —about a hundred dollars total. I borrowed another hundred from my friend Rick and planned an overland trip by bus and train all the way to Western Europe. From there, I would fly to New York. I was invited to stay with an Indian devotee's family in New Delhi for a few days, and then my journey began.

I took a bus from New Delhi to Lahore, Pakistan, then to Peshawar on the western side of the country, and then on to the border of Afghanistan. I crossed the border, traveled over the high mountain Khyber Pass, and on down into Kabul. This is a very memorable road. At its peak you can behold mountain after mountain after mountain—as far as the eye can see. As we crossed, I imagined the history of that pass—Alexander the Great, Genghis Khan, and so many other would-be conquerors had come over this pass with their armies. It was part of the storied Silk Road that connected Asia with Europe. I could almost feel the history as we crossed.

Later that day, when we entered Kabul, I was besieged by a dozen young children, each wanting me to stay at their various hotels. My next bus connection wasn't until six the following morning, so I had to stay somewhere. A young man approached me to say that his brother owned a hotel nearby that was clean and safe and that he himself would guide me back to the bus station the next morning. That appealed to all of my needs, so I went with him. It was one of the rare nights on this journey that I stayed in a hotel. Usually, I looked for night journeys on buses or trains so that I could sleep while I traveled.

The hotel was cheap and clean, but the next morning the young man who had said he would guide me back to the bus station was nowhere to be found. I needed a guide, and I knew that he lived in the hotel. So, I found his room and knocked hard on his door until he got up—reluctantly—and took me to the station.

My memory of Kabul is interesting. This was 1971—eight years before the Russian invasion. When I was there, the country was at peace. Generally, people were friendly and kind; they were inquisitive. I got questions like, "Where are you from?" "What does your father do?" I also got invitations: "Can you come home with me and spend a few days?"

That evening, I sat on a hillside, watching children play in a field below. They were wrestling and flying kites. So many colorful kites were soaring in the air. The feeling in Kabul was different from what I had been experiencing in India. I had purchased a copy of the *Koran* in Bombay to read along the way. I was trying to better understand where I was, and I was particularly interested in the people's religious practices. I was wearing a long, green *kurta*, typical of the area, and I was also wearing a Muslim cap.

*   *   *

The trip across Afghanistan took two days. There were two main routes to choose from. One through the northern part of the country and one through the south. I took the southern route, through Kandahar. At some point in the mid-afternoon of the first day, the bus stopped in a fairly remote area. The bus driver said that it was too hot to continue and that we would resume the journey in a few hours. There was a large mosque nearby, and I walked to it. The front door was locked, so I went around to the side of the building, where there was a shaded outdoor area with tall columns. I went through this area and came to a large courtyard, where a group of forty or fifty men, were forming a circle. In their center, a group of older men began to dance in the circle rhythmically repeating syllables that ended with the emphatic sound of "*HU.*" (It may have been the last part of the Islamic credo, "*La ilaha illa hu*"; however, I really don't know.) They continued to repeat this rhythm as the dance progressed. I was standing in the back of this crowd watching with great interest. This went on for twenty minutes.

As this was going on, I thought I was invisible. I was wearing my Afghan shirt and Muslim cap, and I have a sort of olive complexion that can fit in just about anywhere. Apparently, I was not quite invisible.

Once the dance finished, the entire crowd turned and faced me. "*Musselman? Musselman?*" they began saying to me. I knew they were asking if I was a Muslim. I was twenty-one years old at this time and a bit naïve. I was feeling a sense of unity with them, so my answer was honestly felt. "Yes, Musselman," I said.

Through the crowd whispers began, "Musselman! Musselman!" with great interest.

"Musselman where?" one said, raising his upturned palm and shaking it.

I said, "America."

"Musselman America! Musselman America!" Their voices rolled through the crowd. I was then brought to a mullah and introduced with a few words. I remember his gaze as he looked deep into my eyes. I was told to follow him. He led me behind the mosque, across an area of small houses, to a large, gated residence. There were three or four young boys sweeping the courtyard inside the gate. This felt so familiar—back in the ashram in India, I had performed the very same duties.

The mullah and I and the twenty or so men who were following us went inside and then down some stairs to a hall, maybe thirty by forty feet in size. Around the sides were cushions for sitting. At the front was a slightly raised platform and a small sitting lectern with a book on it. One of the men, an older man, then sat in front of the lectern. It became obvious that there was going to be a reading of the *Koran* or a sermon. Just before it began, a man from the back spoke up with concern in his voice. This went on for a few minutes.

Of course, I didn't know what he was saying, but a few glances in my direction told the story. It was clear there was concern about my being there. I looked over at the mullah seated at the lectern and gestured, pointing to my heart, and then made a waving motion toward the door. He very kindly nodded his head. I left and was met outside by a group of young boys who were instructed to guide me back to the mosque. This was a beautiful experience, and it would seem that I had likely stumbled onto a group of Sufis. It reminded me of my dancing with Sufi Sam in New York. I was very fortunate to have seen this and remember their kind treatment. I was also very lucky that I hadn't inadvertently offended anyone.

*   *   *

The rest of the trip across Afghanistan was fascinating as I crossed what seemed like endless open desert areas. I remember seeing an old man squatting on the side of the road in the middle of nowhere. Was he waiting for someone or something? I could only imagine. We would occasionally stop at a small hut selling food. Being a vegetarian at the time made eating difficult. I mostly ate naan, the traditional flat breads that were everywhere. Once I found a rice dish that had some spinach in it. There was also tea. We followed the road all the way to Herat on the western side and then crossed the border into Iran to the city of Mashhad. From here, I took a train to Tehran and then a bus to Erzurum, Turkey. While on this road we were able to see Mt. Ararat in the distance, rising notably out of flat land all around. This is where some say the biblical Noah's Ark came to rest. From Erzurum, it was a five-hour bus ride north to Trabzon, which is on the Black Sea.

I took a boat across the Black Sea for a student rate of twenty-seven dollars, which covered something they called "deck class." Deck class meant that you were on the back of the boat and on the deck only. No room, no food, and only a deck chair for a bed. It was a two-day trip with four stops along the way for three or four hours each. This allowed me to search for some food and wander a bit in the towns. I visited another mosque as well. The boat's final destination was Istanbul.

Istanbul is a captivating city that was once known as Constantinople. The city is divided by the Bosphorus River, which separates Europe from Asia. I remember the view looking west at sunset over the Bosphorus Bridge. The skyline was full of cathedrals and mosques—a very beautiful sight. I visited a few mosques while I was there and even attended a few services. I respectfully followed the motions and gestures of the other participants. From here I traveled by bus to Athens, Greece. This was a long bus ride, and I probably used it to catch up on sleep.

*   *   *

On this journey, I had planned to make one detour, and that was to Mount Athos, a peninsula in northern Greece that has several different Christian monasteries dating back to at least the ninth century. This land is considered to be holy in the Greek Orthodox faith. I had heard of Mount Athos while I was in India and what I had heard intrigued me. These monks use rosaries and mantra repetition as a major part of their spiritual practices, and I wanted to know more about this.

Getting to Athos required some planning. I had to first go to Athens to get a recommendation from the US Consulate. Then I had to take that recommendation to an office of the Greek Orthodox Church to obtain permits. Getting to Athos from Athens was a journey in itself. While I was planning this, I met Lucas, an older man from Philadelphia, who was going to Athos on a pilgrimage. He offered me a ride for the five-hour drive up the coast to a place where we would then take the two-hour boat ride to Dafni, the port of entry for anyone going to Athos. This was a small open boat, carrying about fifteen people. On the boat, I met a few fellow travelers: two Romanian Orthodox priests from Canada who were on a biblical research project; a man from Guernsey, England; and a young man from Athens, probably in his late teens. The boat also carried a group of six or seven returning monks.

Once we were on Athos, there was a process of presenting our papers at an office in Dafni. I had to meet with a member of the Council of Elders, which was made up of representatives of each of the twelve main monasteries. This person questioned me about my purpose for being there. After interviewing me, he granted me a permit, signed by ten elders, that allowed me to stay for five days.

During my time on Athos, I traveled with the Romanian priests, the young Greek man, the man from Guernsey, and Lucas. We were quite the crew. There were no roads or vehicles between monasteries, so we would hike from one to the other, often an hour or more of walking to each place. And as we walked, we talked. I wish I could remember everyone's name, but the people were memorable. The Guernsey man had a strong cockney accent and a great sense of humor. One of the priests and I shared many religious and philosophical conversations along the way. The young Greek was invaluable to all of us as our translator.

There are about twenty different monasteries with amazing frescoes and artwork that date back to the fifteenth century or earlier. We visited five or six of the monasteries. There were different types of monastic lifestyles, ranging from austere isolation as hermits to communities that had common prayer and practice. The monasteries are mostly Greek Orthodox; however, there was also a Russian Orthodox monastery and a Romanian Orthodox monastery, and I visited these as well. I also saw the ruins of an old Egyptian Orthodox monastery. There is a long history of not allowing women on the peninsula. The monks are fond of saying, "The only woman who has been on Athos in the last twelve hundred years is the Virgin Mary."

Upon reaching each monastery, we would be greeted by a monk whose job it was to welcome visitors. Each monastery apparently rotates this job annually. At each we were offered a shot of ouzo, an anise flavored alcoholic drink, followed by a Turkish sweet and then a small cup of Turkish coffee. This was a bit of a shock to me as I didn't drink alcohol or coffee, and I minimized sweets. However, one could not refuse, and so I managed.

One memory in particular stands out. After spending the night at one of the monasteries, I took a short walk in the morning by myself around the grounds. As I walked around the back, I came upon a sight that surprised me. The corner of the building was open on two sides. In this open room stood neatly piled stacks of human skulls and of arm bones and leg bones. When I went back inside. I asked one of the monks what the bones were for. He told me that when a monk dies, he is buried, and that ten years later, his bones are disinterred and taken to this room. This is done so that the living monks can see what will ultimately happen to their bodies; it is a means to encourage their detachment from worldly life.

At one monastery, there was a monk who seemed particularly friendly. When I asked his name, I was told he was called *If Stratius*, which was translated as "a good soldier." I wondered whether that was his actual name or was it just how he described himself. I began to ask If Stratius about their method of prayer using a bead rope as a rosary. He quietly left the room for a moment and returned, handing me a rosary that was made of wool and that had a woolen cross at the bottom. There were ninety-nine knots tied into this rosary. "Three knots for each of Jesus's thirty-three years of life," If Stratius said. He told me that he did ninety-nine rounds of prayer daily using this rosary. He wrote down the prayer for me in Greek, which I transliterated by the sounds he made, and then later found an English translation for it. The prayer meant, "Jesus Christ, son of God, have mercy on us."

We happened to be at the Romanian Orthodox monastery on a Sunday. The morning vespers began that day at 2:00 a.m., which the Canadian priests and I attended. The chapel was quite small but full of religious icons and altars, some of which appeared gilded. Around the sides were standing cubicles that a person could lean against while sitting on a narrow wooden bench.

In attendance were about five very elderly monks who seemed to be in their eighties or nineties. They sang Gregorian style chants, and their aged voices only added to the timeless beauty of the sacred sound. It was quite an extraordinary experience.

*   *   *

After the five days we were originally allotted on Athos, most of our traveling crew dispersed. The young Greek and I wanted to climb to the top of the mountain that rises over 6,000 feet at the end of the peninsula. To do this we needed an extension of our five-day permit. We managed to get permission for another four days, and we began the climb. Once a year on their holiday of the Day of Ascension, all the monks who could still physically do it, would make the climb to the very small stone church and the six-foot iron cross that stand at the top of the mountain. The Greek boy and I got there late in the afternoon, so we slept on the floor in the church that night and descended the next morning. I may be the only person to have ever recited by heart the *Arati*—a thirty-minute chant that Baba Muktananda compiled in praise of Bhagavan Nityananda —at the top of Mount Athos just before sunset!

By the time we reached the bottom, I was exhausted. We stopped at the Russian Orthodox Monastery for the evening. They welcomed us warmly and fed us well—a hot meal of black bean soup with some fresh bread, which we very much enjoyed. I slept soundly that night but woke up still very tired. However, I pushed on, and we left Athos that day. From here I took a bus to Thessaloniki, where I picked up a train on the Oriental Express route. This route traveled through what was then Yugoslavia, across Austria and finally into Brussels, Belgium, where I was to fly home on an inexpensive student ticket I had purchased in Istanbul. I was increasingly exhausted on this leg of the trip and had no appetite.

When I got to Brussels, however, I was told the flight had changed and was now leaving from Amsterdam. The good news was that there was a bus to take me there. The bad news was that it had left half an hour earlier. I quickly got to the airport and took a twelve-dollar flight to Amsterdam, where I learned the flight to New

York had been delayed. I was given a meal pass and was bussed to downtown Amsterdam, where I had a few hours to wander. I was feeling weak, however, and I could hardly even eat.

Finally, I was on a plane to New York. Then, after a few more buses, I was back at my parent's home in Queens. The entire journey from India to New York took about one month. I had spent a fraction of the two hundred dollars I began with.

The experience was invaluable for me: living for a while in a predominantly Hindu culture, traveling across multiple Muslim nations, experiencing the Greek Orthodox Christian monasteries, and then returning to my Jewish family in New York. I could see commonalities in all of these faiths, yet I had a deep respect for their cultural and philosophical differences. I was comfortable with all of them. No matter where I was, I felt I was in a holy place. One God, many paths.

12. THE ATTIC

I reached my parents' home completely exhausted. I said a few hellos and went to sleep for sixteen hours. When I woke up, I was still exhausted, which caused my mother to insist I see a doctor. She was also shocked to see me so thin. I weighed in at 104 pounds. I'm not sure she ever got over seeing me like that. The doctor took one look at me and said, "Have you seen your eyes?" He held up a mirror, and I saw then that my eyes were canary yellow—a clear symptom of hepatitis. The odd thing was that the bathroom in my parent's house was painted yellow, so I hadn't noticed.

I was immediately taken to the hospital for evaluation. I remembered that while we were hiking around Athos, we all had shared a canteen of water and that one of the Canadian priests wasn't feeling well on his last day with us. Also, we had been drinking stream water much of that time, which was the likely origin of my Hepatitis A, which is sometimes called Travelers Hepatitis. I spent nine days quarantined in the hospital. It was quite surreal when my parents would come to visit me, as they had to be gowned and masked from head to foot. I hadn't seen them in almost a year, and they seemed like ghosts in their gowns. Even with all this I continued to meditate as much as I could in my hospital bed. I would get up early, and timed my meditation to end before the nurses came in on their early rounds.

I spent the next five and a half months recuperating at my parent's house. I was determined to not lose the thread of my practices. I began to meditate, first eight and then ten to twelve hours a day. I would sit for four-hour sessions three times a day: morning, afternoon, and evening. It seemed that my desire for long meditation sessions had to manifest before I could fulfill my guru's commands.

*   *   *

This was clearly a pivotal point in my life, and it was a very fruitful time for me. I took the opportunity very seriously and threw myself wholly into the practices. When I wasn't meditating, I was reading sacred books or doing *japa*, the repetition of a mantra. My meditation quickly became deep and profound.

One day, I was meditating quietly and heard as clear as day, a male voice of heavenly beauty singing the words "*Paraspani Chintaman…*" The last sound of "n" was drawn out in an exquisitely beautiful manner, rising to such sweetness. I had no idea what those words meant. The impression of it stayed with me. Only a few days later I opened a magazine that came from Shree Gurudev Ashram, which mentioned those very words. The *chintamani* is mentioned in both Hindu and Buddhist traditions as "the wish-fulfilling gem."

At one point, while I was meditating—I was fully awake, neither asleep nor daydreaming—the figure of a woman of unearthly beauty appeared beside me. When I say "unearthly," I mean it literally. My mind and memory cannot contain the quality of her immense beauty. She was sitting on the ground on my right with both her legs folded to her left. She smiled and handed me a red rose. In that moment, I felt a sharp pain in my perineum—a piercing sensation—which then proceeded to move slowly up my spine. It felt like a needle, sharp yet benevolent. It stopped at my navel and pulsed there; it moved to my solar plexus, where it again pulsed; it proceeded to my heart, where it expanded into a wide and luminous space; then it continued upward to my throat. This awakened energy was powerful, and now it was moving through me with greater ease.

This had a profound effect on my sadhana, and it set in motion a greater confidence and fervor for my practice. These experiences and many others were powerful indications of the unfolding of Kundalini. A few months later, I was able to read the first English version of Baba's autobiography, *Guru*, which had just been published. I knew that I was experiencing the Kundalini Devi that Baba talked about in his book. I do not believe this to be just some anthropomorphized energy. I have seen the Goddess since—countless other, similar experiences followed.

The process was not always smooth. There were many times when I felt that I was being taken apart and put back together again. Some days, I felt anxious, and I relied on intense prayer to see me through. Sometimes I felt like Sita, the consort of Rama, calling for her Lord. Sometimes I felt like Rama, calling for Sita to join him. Sometimes the energy would rise from the base of my spine; sometimes it would descend from above. I would become troubled if I felt out of touch—I couldn't bear it when I felt disconnected from God. However, I would always push on and continue to persevere with greater intensity. I knew that, ultimately, I was moving in the right direction.

One day as I was meditating, I found myself whisked out of my body into a timeless space. I found myself observing a woman who was standing at a kitchen sink, looking out a window that was in front of her. This woman was a bit portly and was wearing a simple dress. I somehow knew she was a working-class British woman. The sink had indoor plumbing. The kitchen looked as if it was from the 1930s or '40s. I could feel this woman's presence. I knew she lived by herself. She seemed a bit lonely. I then heard a voice, as if from a guide, say, "She was a simple woman, and her tombstone reads, "For God in Eternity." This was a very vivid experience, and at times I have wondered about it. I have searched websites of British tombstones to find this inscription, but I had no luck in finding it.

Once in meditation, I saw a beautiful swan guiding a small wooden boat, which was moving silently through dark, still waters toward a distant light on the horizon. I could see a transparent image of my body, stretched out, projected full length onto this boat. It had no oars and no crew. I knew that the boat was moving by the will of the swan. Its features were focused and sure. I knew that the swan represented Baba, who had been given the title *paramahamsa* by his own guru. *Paramahamsa,* "the great swan," is a term often used to describe a guru of a high order.

I was missing Baba a lot. Often, I would just repeat his name over and over again: "Muktananda, Muktananda, Muktananda!" It became my mantra. Once while I was doing this, I sank deep within myself and visually saw the actual letters MUKTANANDA rising up from my depth. They were rising endlessly with no beginning and no end. I wouldn't know how else to describe it.

*   *   *

After a few months of these experiences, I was inspired to write a letter to Baba. Some months later, I was very surprised to receive a complimentary copy of the 1972 edition of *Gurudevani,* an annual publication of Baba's ashram, where my letter had been printed in full. I never expected it to be anything other than a personal letter. I see now how it reflects my intense longing and devotional state at that time, so I am including it in full here:

A Letter to Gurudev[1]
September 25, 1971

Om Namah Shivaya!

Guru Om, Guru Om, Guru Om. Oh Baba ji, my own true consciousness, my beloved, a thousand prostrations and adorations to thee.

After four weeks of traveling overland, I reached New York City two months ago. The trip was long and difficult, but there were some useful experiences along the way.

By the time I reached home, I was feeling sick, and after seeing a doctor, I was taken to the hospital to be treated for hepatitis. At present I am recuperating at my parent's house.

---

[1] "Letter to Gurudev" is reprinted from the 1972 issue of *Gurudevani* with permission from the SYDA Foundation.

The doctor says I should remain in the house another week or so and that it would probably be one or two months before I could begin to work.

Suddenly being faced with so much free time has been a real test for me; I was concerned that lazy habits of an idle mind might overtake my sadhana, but by your grace, Baba, it has proved quite the contrary. I have been following a strict schedule of practices, which through your loving kindness has proved somewhat fruitful. Along with japa, reading devotional and scriptural material, and rest, I am also sitting for meditation eight to ten hours a day, and much of it seems to be good. I feel I have progressed a great deal. There have been many, many wonderful experiences, and I think my awareness has deepened. Many times, as soon as I close my eyes, I experience great bliss. Often very bright suns appear at *ajna chakra* or *sahasrar*, which at different times seem to emanate light of different moods—sometimes blue or violet, red, green, yellow, white, or black, sometimes rainbow-colored or alternating rays of white and black. Most often it appears whitish or silvery-white.

The *muladhar* [chakra] sometimes feels like a volcano getting ready to explode—light seems to be beginning to shine up from there, and there are often rumbling sensations. I occasionally feel shooting pains at the muladhar or up the right or left side of my torso, or in my head and lower spine.

Throughout a large part of the meditation, I feel subtle rippling movements throughout the spine, sometimes very strongly. Last week a very large white luminous cobra appeared and, with a hood spread wide, gazed directly into me. I often feel the presence of other beings and sometimes see their forms very clearly. Last week while I was having a particularly good meditation, the figure of a man appeared; he was wearing a long brown robe and had a light complexion and a short beard. He looked so familiar to me, but I couldn't place him. I asked him who he was, and there was a brief moment of stillness—his body became slightly transparent, and he began to move upward. I felt I should follow him and found that I could. He seemed to move a little, then wait for me, and then go on. As we went up, a large light came that seemed to be like an entranceway. He went through this and disappeared. I tried to follow him; at first, I thought I was moving through some kind of a bright tunnel with dim objects flying past me—but the next moment I was underneath it again and then the light went away. After meditation, I still remembered very clearly his familiar features, but I couldn't make any connection.

There have been many experiences during sleep and while I was going in and out of the sleep state. A few weeks ago, I dreamed that I was in a crowded hallway, waiting to see a Master. The hall and room reminded me of a typical children's school in America. Everyone seemed to be walking quickly past the Master who, dressed in street clothes, was sitting in a chair facing sideways to me. His head was lowered, eyes closed, and he was slowly rolling back and forth in his seat, seemingly in trance. The line of people moved very quickly, but when my turn came, I knelt and bowed my head to touch his thigh. I uttered *Om Namah Shivaya* with an intense feeling of reverence, and suddenly energy of a tremendous power poured through me. My head was flung backward, hard, and my sahasrar seemed to open up into infinity. I think I lost consciousness for a few seconds. When I came back to consciousness, there was a small ball of sparkling light moving slowly, with intense energy causing a very hard blunt pain, down my right leg, and up again on the inside of my thigh. This light came up as far as my navel on the side and then entered my spine, where the light disappeared. At that point, I woke up. My right leg felt energized for a day or two.

When I first returned home from the hospital, I always felt like falling into sleep after only ten or fifteen minutes of meditation in the morning. (Although even in the hospital, I was awake and meditating by 5:00 a.m.) One morning as I drifted into sleep, I saw myself sitting in a small room with some of the devotees from the ashram. You were seated in front of us on a raised platform. Your body seemed to be covered with tiny scars. Then, with a smile, you pointed to me. I felt very excited. You said, "Don't worry about the headaches and those boils." The next moment I found myself shooting very fast upward through space. I could clearly see what appeared as stars all around me, rushing by fast. This went on for about ten seconds. I was fully aware that I was supposed to be sleeping, yet my consciousness felt as if I were in the waking state. I'm not sure how, but I realized that I could control at will the speed at which I was moving. Suddenly, a large glowing light appeared. It was much larger but not brighter than the stars. A moment later, I realized that I was moving downward at the same speed, and without becoming aware of any change of direction. After a few seconds, I saw, very clearly, clouds moving in from the left. They became thicker and thicker, and I felt that I was moving very fast. In the next second my vision became obscured, and I landed with a tremendous thud, back in my body, which I felt fully. A little bit dazed, I tried to sit up. My eyes were still closed and at that moment, for a few seconds, I clearly saw two blue eyes looking at me. They were larger than life size and almost sparkled with a divine softness. The memory of this experience remained all day.

That night I dreamt I was being given a tour of a rocket testing area. When one of the rockets went up, I seemed to be watching it from above. It went straight up and then down to crash on the earth. I remembered the morning's experience. The guide exclaimed, "Oh, how beautiful!"

The next morning, I again fell into sleep when I suddenly began hearing strange sounds. They became so intense and loud that it was painful and deafening. It was horrifying, Baba! Such noise! The only way I could describe it would be the sound of ten thousand people, screaming with electronic-like voices, while running madly panic-stricken through a dark cavern, being chased by some horrifying demon. I felt that I had somehow penetrated into some sort of hell. This went on for some time. Suddenly the noise got slightly softer, and I clearly heard a voice that sounded like a young boy. He was begging me as if in one more moment he would be killed. "Oh, please let me come up, Steve! Please let me come up. . .Oh, please. . .Please!" Two thoughts came to me at that time. One was that I didn't know who that voice was, and I was afraid. The other was that I wanted to help him. Then I again thought that I wanted to help him, and in that moment, the noise stopped. I heard the voice exclaim in a grateful cry, "Oh thank you, thank you, thank you!" I then saw a sphere of light move from somewhere below the muladhara, up through the spine and enter at the heart.

The next day I was again ready to fall asleep. This time certain guilt feelings were present about going to sleep so often. There was some fear as to what would happen next, but at the same time I was fascinated by these experiences. I tried to ask you in my heart whether I should resist the sleep feeling. Not really quite sure, I succumbed to it. As certain sensations and sounds came, I knew I was going into a strange state. Just then, I had a clear physical sensation of a pair of hands holding the underside of my head. Firmly, yet gently, a voice said, "Get up!" I got up. Since then, I have not fallen asleep very often. Please advise me about this, Babaji. The last day or so, I have again been falling asleep, and again there have been very strange experiences. They are almost always accompanied by an energy of an almost unbearable degree. Sometimes it feels like a welder's torch working in my head, although afterward. I always seem to feel good. Sometimes I feel that these events are uncontrolled, but I know that when things become strange or difficult, as well as when there is bliss, I am protected by your grace.

Baba, there have been so many amazing experiences. I couldn't possibly relate even half of them. Once I saw a beautiful swan silently guiding a small wooden boat through dark waters towards a light in the distance. The water was perfectly still, and there was a dim image of a body, laying down, superimposed on that boat. There was no crew and no oars. The boat moved entirely by the will of the swan. The image of the swan appears at other times as well, and I know that swan is you, Baba.

Sometimes *Shivalingas* appear, or strange luminous objects, pinpoints, and spheres of light of different colors, forest scenes or mountain scenes, or the forms of different deities—particularly Durga, Krishna, and Kali. There are others that I don't recognize. Sometimes I see Sai Baba of Shirdi or Bhagavan Nityananda. The most joy is when I see you. Throughout the day, particularly just before meditation, I see pinpoints of a beautiful blue. Sometimes there are many at once. There is also a small black dot which appears at the beginning of almost every sitting. When the black dot and blue lights appear many times just before or at the very beginning of meditation, I know that the sitting will be particularly good.

Lately, I am beginning to hear sounds. Almost whenever I listen carefully, I hear the tinkling of *kartals*. At times I have heard distant church bells, buzzing like that of a bee, and the sound of a conch, sometimes in short, repeated blasts while at other times in extended tones of various pitch. For the last four days I am hearing what sounds like organ music day and night. There are about five or six notes that just keep repeating themselves in various combinations.

For most of the summer I have been alone, as both my parents work, and my brothers and sister have all been on vacation. Two weeks ago, everybody came home, and things changed considerably. Between the TV, radio, record player, and all the petty arguments that go on, the house is not always conducive to meditation. At first, I was very much disturbed, but I have since moved my place of meditation from my bedroom to the storage attic. It tends to be a little stuffy, and in the afternoons, very hot, but there seems to be much more quiet. At first, I found it difficult to meditate there. There were no spiritual feelings whatsoever, just a dusty and dormant place. Within a short time, however, the whole vibration has been changed, surely by your grace. Now, I feel quite comfortable there.

The day before everyone came home, I was a little worried that due to disturbances, I would not be able to receive meditation. I was praying all day for strength and the ability to be detached. That evening when I tried to fall asleep, I found that I could not—my body was still tingling with energy. After a while, I gave up trying and decided to read for a while. That didn't work either, and I decided to sit for meditation. I began to feel a lot of energy flowing through my body. This continued for a while, and then I felt, and was able to see dimly, a beam of light rising out of my muladhar. It rose up my spine slowly, and when it reached my navel, it remained a few seconds, causing slight quivering motions. It then seemed to pass quickly up through my heart and when it reached my throat, it caused quivering motions that lasted a while. About half of the energy seemed to go on into my head while the rest remained filling the spine up to my neck. After five or ten minutes, it receded. There was continued meditation until almost 2:30 a.m. This same experience has repeated itself quite a few times in the last week. Sometimes it comes only as far as the navel, sometimes to the heart or throat. At the times when it stops at the heart, I also perceive a particular kind of light. It is always accompanied by heat.

There have been a few times when my mind is quiet enough and my concentration is good, when I am blessed with being able to penetrate very deep. Sometimes I ask, "Who am I?" and try to go way back. Other times I try to follow the mantra back to its origin. There were a few times when I went all the way back to a place where a light of silvery white was shining very clear and steady in a background of black, but not darkness. There was a special feeling about it. A certain beauty. Then in front of the light appeared your form, clearly, in seated position; partly transparent and wavering slightly. I felt that this was a special experience. It repeated itself two or three times during that day.

As what I suppose is normal for this early stage of sadhana, there have also been long periods of intense pain and agitation. These experiences have surely been as beneficial as those that bring bliss. A few times while experiencing tormentuous mental pain, I felt at the same time a feeling of bliss. Oh, Babaji, there are still some very foolish mistakes and traps that I fall into repeatedly, which throw me off balance. I am trying hard to let go of them, but without your grace it is impossible. I have learned more deeply during these last few months that there is no amount of sadhana that I can do—even in twenty-four hours a day, for years and years—which could not be accomplished by your grace in an instant. More and more, I realize the value of service in sadhana.

Baba, for a few days last week, every time I would sit for meditation, I would begin to feel more than a little insane. I can't really describe the feeling, but at the same time I was very restless. Sometimes I would burst into tears and call your name uncontrollably. This would last half a minute and then cease. At the time, I couldn't figure out why I was crying. Once, the moment after it stopped, I began to laugh. I didn't know why I was laughing either. Babaji, is this normal for me now? There have been times while sitting when I almost forget who I am and feel like some kind of creature undergoing a bizarre transformation. I know that strange events are expected, but—please, Babaji, please—reassure me about this. Every once in a while, I think that I have perhaps made some mistake and have lost contact with you. Oh, Baba, may that never be! I pray deeply, Baba, that my love for you grows into its full maturity.

When I left Ganeshpuri, you told me to begin to work. I was fully prepared to do so immediately. Now, it seems it will be yet a while before I can do that. Once in a while, the thought comes that I haven't obeyed your instructions, and I don't know what to do. Please advise me about this; I don't want to disobey you. Please tell me what to do concerning my spiritual practices, as well as worldly duties if I am overlooking any. I know that my sadhana cannot bear fruit if I neglect responsibility. Please don't let me get stuck or stagnant, Baba. I am trying the best I know how to open to you more and more. Please be with me and release me from this illusion of bondage! Baba, there are so many things that I would sing to you, but they belong in my heart, not on a piece of paper. I know that you hear them there, perhaps even more clearly than I do.

Oh, Babaji, my dearest Guru, my love, please be with me, and guide me, and strengthen me by your grace. May I have the detachment and the patience to bear these karmas until I am able to fully lay them at your feet.

Oh, my lord, make me worthy of you, and above all, grant me pure love for you. All else is secondary. If it is divine will, Baba, I wish to become a true disciple. Please hear my prayer.

Forgive me if I have taken up your precious time. I think this is the longest letter I have ever written. All I really wanted to say was "I love you." OM.

I did receive a response from Baba, written by Professor Jain, who was Baba's translator at the time. I am including it in full below:

Salutations to Shri Muktananda!

My dear Steve, Jai Gurudev!
You are exceedingly fortunate. You are blessed. Your inner centers have been opened. Baba's grace has performed its most extraordinary miracle. Your experiences are authentic—the true landmarks of the Siddha path. You are firmly set on the way to Self-realization. All that you have to do is to persevere steadfastly with devotion and love for your Guru to ensure that you do not throw away pearls for mere trash. Our heartiest congratulations!

Baba was delighted with your letter, which we received in Delhi. He asked me to read it out to a gathering of over six hundred devotees before his evening discourse. We are very proud of your unfolding.

Be a witness to all the experiences that come. Do not get frightened by the frightening ones or puzzled by the puzzling ones. Baba's grace is with you. It will always protect you. It will unlock all the secrets.

Keep a diary and record all your experiences in it. Write to us from time to time. It does not matter if you cannot resume work for some time. Meditate more and more, as much as you can.

A few clarifications regarding your experiences. What appears as sleep to you is not ordinary sleep; it is the state of tandra, the gateway to different visions and worlds. You must have read about the blue pinpoints (sparks) and the black dot (the black light) in *Chitshakti Vilas*. Alternation of laughter with tears is quite normal. The blue eyes that you see are the eyes of your own form, which you will be able to see clearly in due course.

Babaji is very happy with your love. Keep it up. You are specially blessed. With faith and perseverance, you can certainly attain perfection.

With Baba's blessings,

Prof. Jain

And so, I continued to intensify my efforts. I did record a lot more of my experiences, but after a while I felt that I was paying too much attention to them. After I wrote another ten-page letter to Baba, I tore it up and never sent it. Now, of course, I wish I had that letter to remember those experiences.

After a few more months I had an extraordinary experience, one that is worth describing. As I was meditating deeply, I began to see the sparkling blue pearl of light within me very clearly. This light began to grow brighter and brighter and then expanded to encompass my whole being. It continued to expand until it was a globe of light that encircled my whole body to about three feet all around me. The light continued to expand, and then it disappeared. I was filled with blue light, and the world around me was composed of this light. I was that light. My whole world, inner and outer, was a mere reflection of that light. I came down from the attic, while still in this exalted state. I was ecstatic! I had never felt such an incredible intensity of joy. I felt that all my efforts and my entire life had culminated in this moment. I was fulfilled to an infinite measure. I felt there was nothing more to do or accomplish. I danced a crazy wild dance of ecstasy in my room!

It just so happened that I had a follow-up appointment with my doctor later that very day. I remember seeing the doctor's waiting room and office flooded with the same blue light that was the essence of everything and everyone in it. This state lasted all day. Gradually I returned to a normal state of experience. At the time, it felt like the culmination of my sadhana, but in fact, I still had a lot to learn.

*   *   *

I began to meditate deeper and deeper. I began to become very sensitive to everything. If someone flipped a light switch downstairs, it would reverberate through me even though I was in the attic. I had to prepare my own food as I could no longer eat my mother's cooking. This went on for some time. I understand why some sadhus seek out the quiet of mountain retreats at some points in their inner work. However, I was still unripe in my understanding. There was still quite a lot for me to do. This was a phase. I had to learn to assimilate the world. I believe the greatness of Baba's teaching is that he wants us to be complete in all ways. Again and again, what Baba would say most frequently in his writings and lectures would resonate with me. One such teaching from Baba is that a person—without leaving their home, family, or job—can attain God within their own being.

I remembered reading in the *Isha Upanishad*:

> To darkness are they doomed who devote themselves only to life in the world, and to a greater darkness they who devote themselves only to meditation. They who worship both the body and the spirit, by the body overcome death, and by the spirit achieve immortality.[2]

I wanted that balance, and I believe it's what Baba wanted me to learn.

After a time, I began to have thoughts that, here I was, meditating for long hours in my parents' attic when Baba had told me to drive a taxicab and go back to school. As things progressed, I

---

[2] *The Upanishads: Breath of the Eternal*, pp 27-28, Swami Prabhavananda and Frederick Manchester, Vedanta Society in Hollywood, California, 1957. *Isha Upanishad*, verses 12 - 14

began to feel that I did have a choice about this. I could continue on as I had been and perhaps eventually even leave my body this way. It would be okay. Or I could choose to follow my guru's command.

At one particular moment this choice became clear, and I decided to follow Baba's command. The instant I made that decision, the form of Bhagavan Nityananda appeared. He descended on my right from very high up. His form was tinged blue. He was slim and beautifully radiant in his sitting posture. His presence was powerful. We sat together in stillness for a moment, and then he left. This confirmed my decision and defined my path forward.

The very next day, I went out and applied for a job driving a taxi.

13. Driving a Taxi

1972: This is me, following the Guru's instructions, driving a cab in the Upper West Side in Manhattan.

I never thought that driving a taxi in New York City would give me so great a teaching.

I felt like I was being turned inside out with a demand that I engage more with the world and understand my place within it. The contrast between meditating long hours in the attic and spending all day driving in New York City traffic seemed immense. How could I make this shift? How could I even survive such a contrast? I set out to resolve this challenge, all the time knowing that somehow, if I followed my guru's instructions, I would find a way.

I began to contemplate that the whole universe was within me and that I was in the whole universe as well. As I was meditating, I would say, "Baba, the sun and the moon are your eyes; the earth is your feet. The four directions are your ears. Your stomach is the all-devouring time. You are above me and below me as far as I can think. You are also to my right and my left, in front and behind. You are within me, as I am within you." I don't know where I had heard a version of this prayer before, but it stayed with me.

I continued to rise at 5:00 a.m. and to meditate for an hour in the attic. Then, I would take a bus and subway to the taxi yard, which was near the old Shea Stadium in Flushing, Queens. I would pick up my cab, drive around the corner and park the car. Then I would light some incense and do *puja* to my vehicle from the outside, circumambulating it. I had a photo of Baba in my shirt pocket and a tape player that played *Shri Guru Gita* on the front seat next to me. I then headed across the 59th Street Bridge to Manhattan, where I spent the next eight hours rolling around the busy city streets. When a passenger got in the car, I would turn off my tape player and put on WQXR, the New York classical music radio station. People often commented on how peaceful my cab felt.

Driving taxi is like being in an in-between world. You never go anywhere yourself, but you take other people everywhere. In the course of a day, you are in between so many different lives and activities. One moment you might have a person who treats you pleasantly and respectfully. The next passenger may want to aggressively order you to follow their instructions. The next might be a drunk, who is rolling on the floor of the back seat. One passenger may be quiet, and one may be angry. Once a young man and his companion—who was completely covered with bandages on his head, face, and hands—got in and said, "Never sell bad drugs to a drug dealer!"

Once a young girl got in with a plate full of freshly baked cookies. She began telling me she had just taken LSD for the first time and was on her way to meet her boyfriend. She was very anxious due to her increasingly intense experience, and I spent the whole ride keeping her calm so that she felt safe. When we got to her destination, she said she had to get money from the boyfriend. Of course, she never returned.

One day a man was frantically waving me down. I stopped for him. He opened the door and dove onto the floor of the back seat yelling, "Get me out of here! Take me to the police! Take me to the police!" I asked him what's wrong, and he answered, "They are shooting! They are shooting!" Apparently, he was a security guard at Barney's New York Men's Store. I drove him to the nearest police station a few blocks away and—as he was quite frantic—I went in with him to help him explain. After I described the situation, an apathetic sergeant at the front desk said, "Well you see, the border line of this precinct ends a few blocks from here, so you'll have to take him to this other precinct down the road." Instead, I drove him back to his store to see what was going on. The store manager came out and paid his fare. The poor guy, it was his first day on the job.

One day, I took a woman to her destination, and she said, "Please don't drop me off yet, this is the most peaceful I've felt all day. Can you just drive around for another ten minutes or so?" This happened more than once.

Another day a very elderly and frail woman got in the car and said, "I don't really want to go anywhere. Can you just drive through Central Park for a while? I need to see life."

There are so many taxi stories. Every taxi driver has his own to tell. If a driver meets a colleague, he will inevitably start by saying, "So, a guy gets into my cab yesterday and. . ."

I drove celebrities to their appointments. I took children to school, executives to work, and priests to their duties. This went on and on, day after day. All this happened while my taxi was rolling around the busy, grimy streets of the city. It was not always a pleasant experience. Sometimes. I would be extremely disheartened by my thwarted desire for peace and quiet. The contradictions were sometimes excruciating. However, I knew I had to absorb it all. Some days were good, and some days were very difficult. Sometimes as I was driving, the whole city would turn into blue light. At those moments an extreme bliss would be coursing through me. Turning the steering wheel became ecstatic, stepping on the brake was ecstatic. I felt such elation as I became absorbed in blue light—even while I was totally focused on my driving.

At other times the city would look like Mother Kali in her most terrible aspect. It looked like everyone was being chewed up and spit out. People looked gray, crippled, unhealthy, and unhappy. The streets looked dirty. Everything seemed to be a severe energy drain. This was tortuous to me, and I would begin to pray for relief.

I was returning home one day after a difficult day at work and began to feel very separated from the best of my experience. I began to internally call out to the universe. I remembered a prayer from a poet-saint:

O Lord, you who hear the pitter-patter of the feet of the ants, please hear my prayer.

In a similar manner, I was saying to God. "How is it possible for me to be separate from you? You are everywhere and you're in everything— including me! Why can't I see this?" I was walking down the street at the time, and I grabbed hold of a telephone pole I was passing. "Aren't you in this pole as well? Why are you hiding? You have to reveal yourself to me!" With this, I began to feel calm once again.

One day while meditating in my attic, I was feeling intensely out of sorts and not looking forward to spending the day driving taxi. Suddenly, the form of the Vajreshwari Mountain near Ganeshpuri appeared to me. Vajreshwari Devi herself then floated off the top of the mountain, entered me, and began spinning, going faster and faster within me She spun around like a tornado and then exited out of the top of my head lifting all the anxious negativity out of me. I was left feeling relaxed, blissful, and peaceful.

*   *   *

During the day, I would continue to contemplate that the entire city was within me, as I was in the entire city. I would contemplate that the fullness and peacefulness of my inner experience was still within me. Where else could it be? When I was in the attic meditating, I would contemplate that the noise and bustle of the entire city was present within me. I remembered a passage from the *Bhagavad Gita*:

> He who sees inaction in action and action in inaction is wise among men. He is a Yogi and has performed all actions.[3]

I began to allow myself to be bigger than any outer experience. I strove to absorb all the noise, all the feeling of the streets, all the varied forms of people I met. Noises could no longer bother me. While on the subway traveling to work, an express train would often speed through on the center tracks without stopping. Anyone who has ever ridden a New York City subway has experienced the intense and excruciatingly loud roar. I would allow that sound to pass through me as I absorbed and assimilated the force of the energy. I was larger than that sound. I had to be.

At noon, I would sometimes park on Times Square, where there was a taxi stand on the site of the present day Ticketron. As it was lunch hour, there would be many thousands of people on the street. I would lock the cab doors, sit in lotus posture on the front seat, and meditate. I would absorb the sounds of horns honking and people yelling. People would be banging on the cab's windows and doors. "Hey, wake up in there!" "Hey Buddy, I need a cab!" I was oblivious to them. I would actually have deep meditations.

Oh my God, I can't believe I actually did that, and more than once. If you ever see a cabby doing this, please be patient. I know how crazy this all sounds, but there I was. I definitely don't recommend this as a meditation technique!

*   *   *

---

[3] *Bhagavad Gita* 4.18. *The Bhagavad Gita*, p75. Sri Swami Sivananda, Divine Life Trust Society, 1968.

Day by day I saw the best and the worst of life. It was an amazing education overall, and I don't know how else I could have gained the perspective I got from driving taxi in New York City. I saw that our day-to-day choices determine our daily experience and the trajectory of our lives. I saw that life can go a lot of different ways. I felt blessed and protected.

I was driving very late one night when a young man flagged me down on a quiet street on the Lower East Side. He seemed quite distraught. He told me that his good friend was very sick and needed a ride home. Saying that he'd be back in a minute, he ducked inside one of the doors. Just before he returned, an older man emerged, wearing a long dark coat, a black fedora hat, and carrying a small, black case. He looked around suspiciously and scurried away. The young man then came out with a young girl assisted by another young man. She was clearly quite drunk. As they got in the cab, it seemed obvious that she had just had an abortion. The two young men were noticeably upset. It was so sad to see this. That image of a "back-alley abortion" has stayed with me all these years. In today's world this becomes even more relevant. A woman should have safer options.

On my days off, I would often go into Manhattan and wander from church to church, synagogue, or any other place that seemed holy. I would sit in one place, meditate quite peacefully for some time, and then move on to the next place. In one church in midtown Manhattan, I found a small pamphlet written by a French monk, Brother Lawrence, called *The Practice of the Presence of God*. This inspired me greatly as it described what I had been doing.

One day, while feeling terribly distraught, I walked into St. George's Church in Flushing, Queens. I sat down to meditate and quite unexpectedly, as I closed my eyes, an angel appeared. This celestial being was male, very strong, very focused, and very compassionate—and, yes, he had wings. Big, strong masculine wings. Behind him and off to his right was a younger angel, also with wings, who appeared to be an apprentice. The stronger angel touched me, and whatever anxiety I was experiencing dissolved—

completely and immediately. It was just one more out of so many blessings.

*   *   *

While all this was going on, a New Yorker named Ira, who had met Baba Muktananda on his first world tour, was hosting satsangs on the Upper East Side of Manhattan. Baba had told Ira to invite people to come to his apartment for meditation. I used to go there after work, along with Nandini Weizmann and a few other of Baba's students. I always stopped at a fruit stand outside the subway station on Lexington Avenue and 86th Street to pick up an offering of fruit to bring. I would wave the fruit in the air, mentally offering the fruit to God, as I walked to Ira's. One day as I did this, a form appeared as if through an opening in time and space. This form was a divine blue being, perhaps ten feet up in the air and larger than life. My eyes were open. This being was bedecked with jewels and had the sweetest smile. He was incredibly beautiful—beyond anything my mind could imagine. Even my memory cannot contain the beauty of this being's form. He reached out his arms and mentally accepted the fruit and then disappeared. Afterward the fruit felt like it was glowing in my hands.

Ira was quite eclectic in his spiritual interests. He was deeply involved in Sufism—a practitioner and a serious scholar of the tradition—and he had written a book on the whirling dervishes of Turkey. On different nights he had different groups meeting at his house, alternating satsangs of various teachers. Someone wrote to Baba and told him this, and Baba then suggested that there should be a more focused group for his own students.

I was planning on returning to Ganeshpuri at this point; however, a woman by the name of Mira came back from India with a message from Baba. She was given a pair of Baba's sandals and told to start a meditation center to be called the Siddha Yoga Dham of New York. Baba had taught Mira how to do puja to Baba's sandals. She had been told to ask Michael and me for help. Michael lived in

Oneonta, New York, which is about five hours north of New York City, so it was up to me to help Mira. The problem was that she lived in Co-Op City, a section of the Bronx a good forty-five minutes from Manhattan by subway. We held the first satsang at her apartment with Mira, two of her friends, and me. We chanted, meditated, and performed puja. At one point Mira had to be out of town for ten days and was concerned that she couldn't do the prescribed daily puja as she had been directed by Baba to do. She gave me the sandals, and while she was away, I kept them in my attic doing the necessary pujas.

However, no one was really attending this satsang. It was too far away from Manhattan, which is where most people lived. It was obvious that something had to change. The center was then moved to the apartment of a man named Bernard on West End Avenue on the Upper West Side of Manhattan. We met there for a few months, with about fifteen participants, until Bernard and his wife decided to separate. That resulted in his moving out of state. We needed a more permanent place to meet.

Nandini Weitzman, who also lived nearby, offered her apartment on 95th Street and Broadway. This is where Siddha Yoga Dham of New York really took off. Many people began coming, and it became a wonderful welcoming place for Baba's devotees to meet. As I remember, we met twice a week at that time. We had a full house every week. Nandini and I became good friends, and I even slept there two nights a week after satsang, most often in the top bunk of her son Charney's bed. I would then go to pick up my taxicab in the morning and go straight to work. There were many devotees, new and old, who came there regularly. Great people, great satsangs, great chants. I relished the experience there. The Siddha Yoga path finally had a home in New York. Nandini really shepherded the growth of the satsang that ultimately resulted in the creation of an independent ashram at its current location on 86th Street. New York owes her a great debt of gratitude for this.

PART THREE—INTEGRATION

.

14. RETURN TO INDIA

Before I could return to Ganeshpuri, I had to fulfill one more instruction that Baba had given me. He had told me to take classes. Only after I had enrolled in an anthropology class at Queens College and got an A did I feel ready to return to India. I sent a Western Union telegram to the ashram requesting to come. I was told to meet Baba in New Delhi, where he would be on tour. I made my preparations.

I wanted to bring something to Baba as a gift. I decided on a beautiful purple orchid to which I attached a tiny photo of his guru, Bhagavan Nityananda, at the center. With Mira's help, I fixed a few peacock feathers as a backing. To me this represented the guru as the center of all beauty and life. I packaged this floral offering carefully to protect it. The airplane happened to have a layover at the airport in Beirut, Lebanon, and we had to deplane for a few hours. I was concerned as to how to preserve the orchid from the heat, so I took it over to a food counter and asked the server if she could please put it in their refrigerator for a while. She looked at me very seriously and refused. Naively, I hadn't thought about the political situation in Lebanon in 1972. Perhaps she thought I wanted to plant an explosive device.

Finally, I arrived in New Delhi. When I got there, I was told that Baba had left two days before and was visiting devotees in Gujarat State. As I remember, the town was Medhasan. I traveled for four or five hours by train and bus from Delhi to meet Baba.

Baba was staying in a large house near a lake. When I arrived, I was able to see him right away. I presented my orchid and was certainly wondering about its condition as I didn't dare open it during the long journey. My offering had made it, but it didn't look quite as vibrant as when it was packaged. Baba took it and smiled as he saw the photo of his guru in the flower. He took off the peacock feather backing and placed it by Bhagavan's photo on his table. Baba was very sweet and told me to stay with him for the rest of his Gujarat tour. Two other Westerners, a couple from Australia, were being sent back to the ashram in Ganeshpuri. I was now the only person touring with Baba who was not from India. We traveled throughout Gujarat State for the next two weeks. During this time, I mostly rode with Amma in her car. Amma was always like a grandmother to me, even on Baba's first world tour. She was always there to answer a question or to give advice. I was very pleased to be riding with her.

Nothing was being translated for me, but I was fascinated to watch Baba meeting with his devotees. Once we stopped on the side of a road in front of a simple hut where a woman came out to see him. Baba greeted her with so much love. She did a simple puja to him and offered him sweets. She was overjoyed to be doing this. I was told that Baba knew her from his sadhana days.

We then drove on to the next stop in a small town where a large tent had been erected in its center especially for Baba's visit. Baba gave a talk amid flowers, food, and festivities. We were there for just a few hours before driving on. After this we stopped at a very large home that had once been occupied by a local maharaja. Only a small portion of the home was now being used by the maharaja's son or grandson, but still, you could feel its opulent history. We stopped there for a sumptuous lunch. We also made stops in the major cities of Gujarat where there were established Siddha Yoga centers, including Ahmedabad, Surat, Baroda, and others. This is how it went for two weeks. We spent time in one place and then in another —a few minutes, a few hours, or even a few days.

At one stop we were in a hall filled with fifty or more people. I was sitting in the back when Baba said something directed at me. People turned to look at me. One devotee translated for me: "Baba says you should tell some of your experiences." This was so unexpected that I just froze. I was stunned as I had never spoken about my experiences to anyone with the exception of that long letter I had written to Baba many months before. I was so surprised that I really couldn't speak. After a long pause, Baba said, "Ah, he can't say anything because I haven't given him permission to speak yet." I think he may have said that just to save me. I felt I had let him down, but I just wasn't ready.

We finally reached Baroda, Gujarat, which was the home of Dalatubhai Desai, a dentist and well-known devotee of Baba's who regularly made the five-hour journey to Ganeshpuri. We spent a few days in Baroda before returning to Ganeshpuri. A few devotees from the ashram joined us here, and we had evening satsangs and chanting sessions as a delightful finale to Baba's tour.

*   *   *

Getting back to my beloved Ganeshpuri at last was wonderful! I bowed in the street at the front steps as I had done mentally for the past year while in America. As I did so, the marble steps themselves became alive to me. They seemed as flexible and soft as skin. I felt the ashram was Baba's very form. I was very happy to be home.

Life settled in as I adapted to the daily routines of the ashram. I now offered seva in the main temple and in the front courtyard at the ashram's entrance. This was a busy location, with people coming and going all day long. During chanting times in the temple, I would pass out chanting cards or books with the English transliterations of the words to the chants. Before special occasions, we would polish the brass of the window and door ornaments. Baba always wanted everything to be perfect. I remember one day, after we had spent three days cleaning and polishing, Baba walked into the temple to inspect. He walked directly over to a back window, picked up a small paperclip on the ledge, and said, "What's this?" We all were surprised and somewhat amused. We did take it seriously though, and we quickly and carefully looked at all the window ledges.

Baba seemed to know everything about us. It often felt like he knew every thought we had as well as our entire history. Once someone asked him, "Baba, are you reading my mind?" Baba looked at him and made a face of disgust. He said, "Why would I want to read your mind?" That put an end to the question, and we all laughed a bit. Sometimes, however, it appeared to be true. It seemed that Baba was reading our minds. It had been my habit to begin my meditation by repeating Baba's name—Muktananda, Muktananda, Muktananda—as if to invoke his presence. Sometimes that would be my entire meditation. Early one morning, as I left the meditation veranda, I heard Baba's voice in the dark of the courtyard say something to me. Noni Patel—Baba's attendant, who years later became Swami Sevananda—was with Baba and translated, "Don't repeat my name; repeat the mantra." I took his message to heart. But how did he know what I was repeating silently to myself? Clearly, Baba was aware of us at a very deep level. Sometimes his name still resounds in my heart along with the mantra.

On weekends, there were hundreds, sometimes thousands, who would come from Bombay and its surrounding areas to visit Bhagavan Nityananda's samadhi shrine in the village of Ganeshpuri. They frequently stopped at Shree Gurudev Ashram for Baba's darshan and to tour the ashram gardens, which were well known for their beauty. I loved the chanting and the ashram routines. I meditated when and where I could but was kept very busy cleaning and managing the crowds. I slept in the men's dorm above the temple.

*   *   *

In the last week of December 1972, my friend Bill Stucky, whom I had known from Hilda Charlton's group and Baba's retreats at Big Indian, New York, invited me to attend the wedding of a young man named Saumil, in Bombay. The bridegroom was the son of a Bombay devotee who visited the ashram regularly. Bill arranged for us to stay at the home of Maurice Frydman, whom he had previously met through another devotee. Maurice was an engineer from Poland who spent his later life in India. He had been a strong supporter of Mahatma Gandhi and spent time living in his ashram. Maurice had designed, built, and improved the spinning wheel that Gandhi himself used throughout his campaign for India's independence. Gandhi did this to show how small cottage industries could be developed in India to decrease reliance on cloth made in England. Maurice had also spent time with Ramana Maharishi, a well-respected Indian holy man, and he was currently working closely with Nisargadatta Maharaj, another Indian guru. Maurice had translated Nisargadatta's widely read book, *I Am That*, into English. Maurice treated the two of us very well, and we spent a pleasant evening with him. While we were there, Bill got a phone call from Mr. Nagpal, a trustee of Baba's ashram in Ganeshpuri. Bill was told that he and I should go to the main Bombay train station early the next morning to welcome the Karmapa, who was the sixteenth head of the Kagyu Tibetan Lineage and was coming to visit Baba in Ganeshpuri. We were told to welcome the Karmapa and bring him back to the ashram.

The Karmapa's train rolled into the station at sunrise on New Year's Day 1973. We had a few moments of greeting and welcoming him. The Karmapa was quite an impressive being, even there in the busyness of a train station. There was a chair fitted on the steps leading to the train car, and for a few moments, the Karmapa sat there while people came up to show their respects.

We then escorted this holy man to the home of Didi Contractor, in Juhu Beach, where snacks and refreshments were served prior to our trip to Ganeshpuri. The Karmapa's presence was very strong. I remember that I wasn't feeling well that day. Perhaps something from the wedding feast the previous day hadn't agreed with me. I began to feel uneasy, and I was also missing Baba. I glanced up at the Karmapa, and he looked at me directly. He then turned his gaze to a photograph of Baba on the wall. As my gaze followed his to the photo, I felt a sudden surge of energy from the image of Baba, and my unease was completely lifted. I really respected that the Karmapa had relieved me of that unease by diverting my attention to Baba's photo instead of helping me directly.

The Karmapa stayed in the ashram overnight and performed his Black Crown ceremony in the main temple. This was the first time, he had done this highly respected ceremony outside of Sikkim, where he had been living. Baba seemed quite fond of him and spoke very highly of his state.

*   *   *

Every day was centered around Baba and his daily schedule. He was my focus and my purpose. I didn't really have time or interest in building friendships, and I kept pretty much to myself when I wasn't offering seva. I think this bothered a few of the other men in the dorm. They likely saw me as standoffish and too intense. I was aware that there were three or four men who resented me for this. In retrospect, I could have done more to cultivate camaraderie with them, but they were occasionally insensitive and I saw this as unkind and unnecessary. I believe they saw my strict adherence to sadhana as something of a reproach to their more relaxed attitude toward their practices. I always sat up in my bed for a few minutes of meditation before sleep and also upon awakening at the 3:30 a.m. bells. It was my way of starting and ending my day with remembrance of my purpose. One fellow named Ram would say, "Why don't you go to sleep? Have you been meditating all night?" I wished that I had been, but I would let his comments slide past me without response. If Ram saw me, sitting at the front of the temple in the small courtyard after the lunch break, he would sneer at me as he headed to the tea shop. He would say, "Why don't you go for f*** g tea?" Ram would be bleary-eyed, having just gotten up from a nap. I would have loved a tea, but I couldn't leave my post. This was somewhat hurtful, but I just ignored him.

*   *   *

In late 1973, Baba announced that in a few months he would be going on a second world tour. He told many of us to return to our hometowns and prepare for his visit. For me that meant going back to New York City. Many of us started to make our plans to leave India. Ram and Larry, who was another of the crew from the Sadhu Dorm, were also heading to New York, but they made it very clear that they didn't want to be on the same plane with me. I went to Bombay by myself to get airplane tickets. It turned out that we were all on the same plane. The two of them had arranged a ride to the airport and, although there was room for another in their car, they insisted that I not accompany them. I found my own ride. I didn't know why they were behaving like this, and, as I've said, I found it hurtful.

On the day of our flight, I went to the ashram's front gate, where I saw Ram and Larry with a small crowd of people who were making a big fuss over their departure. There were lots of hugs, and people were giving the two of them garlands and boxes of sweets. Gopal Desai, the ashram manager, was making it quite celebratory.

Seeing all of this, I felt that I just couldn't leave the ashram with such a feeling of exclusion. I dropped my backpack and ran back into the main courtyard. To my surprise and delight, Baba was sitting in his seat. There was no one else with Baba except Rajendra, a young man from Delhi who lived in the ashram and worked in the courtyard with me. He spoke perfect English.

I ran up to Baba and bowed. He spoke to me with great affection for quite a few minutes, and, since Rajendra was there, Baba's words to me were translated. On the plane I wrote down what I could remember of this farewell darshan.

> Man's mind becomes attached to many things in this world, and as a result, he carries around his own self-created heaven or hell. But a man whose mind becomes attached to the guru's feet, he becomes immortal. There is nothing that can't be accomplished by such a one. All things are possible for him. . . .

There are two spiritual viewpoints in this world: one is positive and one negative. The negative says, "I am the lowest of the low, smaller than small," but the man of vision sees his own greatness and realizes his own divinity.

Raising his index finger to my face, Baba went on:

Attain that vision! . . .

Nityananda has done good for thousands upon thousands, more than you can imagine. . . .God's universe blossoms downward, Nityananda's universe blossoms upward. . . . Do not belittle yourself. Attain awareness of your true divinity.

My blessings are with you.

Baba then handed me an apple and told me to eat it on the plane, saying, "*Abi jao!*" (Go now!)

When I got to the plane, I found that not only were Ram and Larry on my flight, but we were all seated next to each other in the same row. I was fine with that. I was still in bliss with the afterglow of Baba's words. I understood that when Baba spoke about how "God's universe blossoms downward," he was talking about how infinite Consciousness contracts and descends to become this multifaceted world in which we, as human beings, become involved and forget our divine origin. And when he spoke about how "Nityananda's universe blossoms upward," he was saying that through the grace of the guru—and by pursuing meditation and other spiritual practices—seekers can blossom upward toward recognition of our true, divine nature.

With great reverence I ate the apple Baba had given me, right down to its core. I found seven seeds in that apple, and I still have those seeds today. My ashram farewell was so much better than any garland or box of sweets, which I suspect are now long gone. Fifty years have passed, and I am still enriched and enlivened by Baba's words to me.

15. THE SECOND WORLD TOUR: DRIVING BABA

1974: Here, I am driving Baba in Piedmont, California, in April.

The American leg of Baba's second world tour began in Northern California in April of 1974. Baba stayed in Piedmont at the home of Don Harrison, a dealer in Eastern antiques. At that point, Don Harrison and David Pierce were the two tour managers in the US. A few of Baba's immediate staff also stayed in Don's home with Baba. Various lectures and satsangs were scheduled throughout the area.

A group of seven or eight of Baba's students from New York flew out to join the tour on the West Coast. We rented a house about a half mile from where Baba was staying. There were morning chants and meditation at Baba's house. We walked back and forth between our place and Baba's many times during the day, just to help out in any way we could. One day I received a message that Baba was asking for me. I ran over to his house as quickly as I could. I was greeted by Don Harrison and Eddie Oliver and was told that Baba was in the process of choosing someone to be his driver.

Don said, "Baba, you can have Eddie or Steve"—though Don clearly wanted Eddie because he had lived in California and was familiar with the roads.

Baba walked over to me and put his arms around my shoulders. Baba said, "He's a very good driver; he's my driver."

I was elated of course. It was four years since Baba had first told me in New York that I would be his driver and travel with him all over India. I did travel with him in India but not as his driver. So, Baba was keeping his promise. I was thrilled that he remembered this after four years. I now moved into Baba's house and slept in the basement with a few other devotees who were serving the guru directly.

*   *   *

Driving for Baba seemed like a natural role for me after all the practice I'd had driving a taxi in New York City. Baba's car was a small Mercedes. I took great pride in washing the car and preparing it for his outings. I drove Baba everywhere, usually with Professor Jain, who served as his translator during the first half of the tour. Baba would sit in the back seat. Jain would sit up front with me. It was common after an outside lecture for Professor Jain to stay behind to answer people's questions, and then I would drive Baba home alone.

I had to be totally focused when driving Baba. After his presentations, which always ended with meditation, he would be incredibly radiant, and his energy would fill the car so strongly. I kept a pack of Life Saver candies in my pocket so that I could ground myself at those times. Sometimes on a long drive, I would look in the rearview mirror and be amazed to see Baba sitting there.

He would often be doing japa or singing to himself. Sometimes, to stretch his legs, he would put his feet up on the front seat bench which was just a few inches from my head. Here I was, Baba's feet next to my head, Baba himself in the back seat, and it was just the two of us out on the open road. It just doesn't get any better than that!

Sometimes, Baba would read highway signs to practice his English. One afternoon when we were driving over the Oakland Bay Bridge, Baba was stumped when he saw the word "Oakland." He was sounding out the letters slowly, one at a time, and then he asked me what it said.

I said, "Oakland, Baba."

"Oakland?" he exclaimed with some amazement. This was followed by a long string of words in Hindi, which I didn't understand.

*   *   *

Baba liked me to drive fast. He was never a time waster. Once we were leaving a lecture at the Scottish Rite Masonic Center in San Francisco. It was getting late, probably around 9:00 p.m. We were on a big street without any other cars. There was a sequence of at least five traffic lights just ahead of us that had just turned yellow. Baba tapped me on my shoulder and said, "Make the light!" I stepped on the gas, and we clicked off each of those lights just as they were turning red.

Once we were driving back to Piedmont from a weekend retreat at Redwood Glen, which was about two hours away. The final session of the retreat had gone a little over, so we had gotten a late start on our drive. I knew we were expected back at the house by 11:00 a.m. as Baba was scheduled to meet then with a special guest. I was driving along, going probably 85 or 90 miles per hour and traveling in the fast lane. This was usual on the open highway for us at that time. A car pulled alongside us in the next lane with a few devotees in it. They matched our speed and were happily waving to Baba.

Baba rolled down his window and waved back, calling out in English, "I love you."

This, of course, made the devotees even happier. Then one of them—Shankar, who was sitting in the back seat of their car—began egging on the driver, Gargi. Shankar was hitting Gargi on her back, saying, "Pass him, pass him!" Gargi looked a bit scared, but she put her foot on the gas and the other car passed us by.

There was a long pause in the back seat of our car, and then Baba tapped me on the back and told me, in English, "Pass them!"

So, I put the gas pedal to the floor, and the Mercedes took off with gusto. We easily passed the other car, and I kept up our high speed until they had disappeared behind us.

I then slowed down a bit, and we continued on home. As we pulled into the driveway at the Piedmont house, I looked down and noticed it was 10:58 a.m.—two minutes before Baba's scheduled meeting. I told Baba that we had made it in time for his meeting but that I'd had to drive around a hundred to do it."

Baba asked, "Miles per hour or kilometers per hour?"

I said, "Miles, Baba."

He then asked, "What is the speed limit?"

This was 1974, the year that all highway driving in the US had been reduced to 55 miles per hour. I told him that, and he responded by exclaiming, "Waahh! Waahh! Waahh!" while tapping his head. He then said, "Just drive 75, and you'll be OK."

I must have looked at him with some concern, because then he said, "Look, just drive slightly faster than the cars around you and don't do anything obvious." It would seem he had just mastered the art of highway driving.

One night we were driving home from an evening lecture. It was just Baba and me in the car. It was late, and I knew he wanted to get home. There was no traffic to speak of, and I was in the left lane. I passed another car on the right and noticed, a bit too late, that it was a police car. I kept up my speed until I was safely past him, and then

I moved into the right lane and slowed down to match his speed. How would he respond? It didn't take him very long to put on his siren and pull me over. I got out of the car and walked over to him.

The policeman asked me, "Who do you have there?" I told him he was a visiting dignitary from India. I added that it was late and that I wanted to get him home. The policeman put his foot up on the back bumper of Baba's car and politely said, "Son, you are just going to have to be more conscious on the road."

He was right about that! He gave me a ticket. When I got back into the car, Baba said, "Ticket?" in a sweet voice in English.

I did start driving more slowly after that. For the next few weeks, we could be driving along a highway, and Baba would hit me on the shoulder and say, "Uncle." I knew that in India, a wife's brother is an authority figure in her marriage. The uncle sees that his sister is treated properly, so that children of that marriage grow up knowing that their uncle is someone to pay attention to. I knew that by "uncle," Baba meant the police were nearby. I would drive around the next bend, and there would be a police car waiting for speeders. There was no way that the car could possibly have been seen from our prior vantage point. This happened a few times, but I was already driving within the speed limits.

*   *   *

On one occasion, we stopped in San Jose at the home of Kersi Bulsara, later known as Swami Gurupremananda. Kersi had a small meditation group there, and he was very fond of Baba. There was an informal group of ten or fifteen people present at the time. One young woman asked Baba, "How do you think history will remember you?"

It was extremely rare for Baba to comment on future events in this way, but that day he did. He had a faraway look in his eyes for a moment, and then, speaking slowly, he said, "In three hundred years, they will say a great man came."

We were all intrigued by this.

The young woman then asked: "Will Jesus ever walk the Earth again?"

Baba said, "It is entirely possible." He paused and then said, "However if he does, he will tell you to meditate on yourself, honor yourself, as God dwells within you as you."

*   *   *

We held a few weekend retreats at Redwood Glen, south of San Jose and about two hours from Piedmont. As Baba's driver, I would go to as many programs as I could but at the end, I always left a few minutes early to get Baba's car ready for him. On the final day of the last retreat, I pulled up in his car and heard the sounds of an ecstatic chant going on in the main hall. The pitch was getting louder and louder when I heard Baba's voice shouting loudly. I later asked what was going on and was told Baba stood up out of his chair and brought the chant to a feverish pitch, yelling, "No more suffering!"

When Baba got into his car this time, I felt something was different. The energy was so powerful that I felt as if a living lightning bolt had gotten into the car. He was completely silent all the way to a stop we were scheduled to make at the Siddha Yoga Meditation Center in Santa Cruz. At the center, Baba gave a brief talk outside in the yard and held darshan. The air was electrified. Something felt different. Baba seemed more indrawn than usual. He was completely silent as we continued on to Piedmont.

The next morning about ten of us did a recitation of *Shri Guru Gita* at Baba's house. He came downstairs and sat with us afterward. He looked tired, and his valet, Noni, also looked exhausted. Noni said that Baba had been up all night in pain. Baba told us that he had given a great many people shaktipat the day before and that he'd had to burn off so much of their karma. He said it was like fire in his body.

Bruno, who was one of our group, asked, "Can you transfer some of that to us, so we can help?"

Baba said, "You wouldn't be able to handle it."

It was clear to me then just how much Baba sacrificed himself to awaken so many.

*   *   *

At one point Baba was invited to be a keynote speaker at a conference in San Diego. He asked me how long it would take to drive there. We were in Pasadena, California, at the time. I had already looked at the trip on a map, and I told him it would take three hours and fifteen minutes. Baba said, "Let's drive." David Pierce, the tour manager, wasn't happy. He had already purchased tickets for Baba to go by plane. David said it wasn't possible to get there in that amount of time and that it would take much longer. I sensed that Baba wanted to drive as he usually enjoyed seeing the scenery of the surrounding areas—but he gave in to David and agreed to fly.

I drove the car alone and met Baba at the San Diego airport. The first thing he asked as he got in the car was, "How long did it take you to drive here?"

I told him, "Three hours and ten minutes, Baba."

Baba turned to David and lovingly patted him on the head, saying, "You have to meditate more. Just repeat Baba Nityananda, Baba Nityananda."

David was embarrassed, and he flushed a bit at Baba's words. I confess that I was feeling quite satisfied. This incident did not, however, put me in good stead with David.

A few weeks later, we were driving home from a lecture. Bruno was leading in Amma's car, and I was driving behind him with Baba. David was with me in the front seat of Baba's car. I saw Bruno begin to get off the highway at the wrong exit. I had to make an instant decision: did I follow Bruno's mistake, or did I go on to the next exit as we had planned? At the last second, I decided to follow Bruno, and so I—quite safely—crossed a few feet of the white lines that designated this exit. Bruno then found his way, and we arrived home without incident.

A few days later, I got a message from David that I wasn't to be Baba's driver anymore and that I should give the keys to Bheema. David implied that this was because of my driving. I felt, of course, that this was unfair. Bheema drove Baba for most of the rest of the tour.

The next day, Baba was to speak at a small religious school where he had been invited by a young priest he'd met. This was the first outing in a while on which I was not his driver. I was very disheartened. I had gone to the talk in another car along with a few other devotees, and when we arrived, I went outside to sulk a bit. There was a light fog that fit my mood. After a while I went into the school to hear Baba's talk. One of the first things Baba said after I came in was, "Being with the guru doesn't mean sitting in his hip pocket. It means following his teachings."

This, of course, hit home for me. It was hard to swallow, as I had formed a strong identification with the role of being Baba's driver. However, I had to let it go, and I did.

16. The Second World Tour Moves On

After a few weeks, I was asked to go on to Denver, Colorado, with Rick to set up Baba's tour in both Denver and Boulder. We were there for a month before Baba's arrival. There were lecture halls to find, places for Baba's entourage to stay, and many other necessary preparations to make. We stayed at Rick's parent's house in Denver. It just so happened that his parents lived next door to where a young Indian man named Guru Maharaji was living. After gathering many followers, he had recently stepped down from his position as guru and married. I confess that Rick and I sometimes looked from behind a curtain at an upstairs window to watch Guru Maharaji in his backyard, mowing his lawn and playing in his pool. It seems this young man had created quite a stir in the Denver community by running around town in his various sports cars. The local press had been pretty hard on him. As a result, interest in "another guru" in Denver was quite a bit dampened.

Rick and I were also planning satsangs for Boulder, about an hour from Denver in the foothills of the beautiful Rocky Mountains. The Naropa Institute was in Boulder. Today, it has grown into the fully accredited Naropa University. As I approached the front door at Naropa, I met Allen Ginsberg, the well-known poet. We stopped to talk for a few minutes, and I invited him to meet Baba. He readily agreed. A plan was made for Baba to speak at Naropa, and Allen Ginsberg was to give the introduction. The Naropa Institute was closely affiliated with the Tibetan Buddhist teacher Chogyam Trungpa, who was its founder. Chogyam Trungpa also established a Buddhist community in Boulder known as the Karma Dzong, and most of his closest students were participants. The Karma Dzong was in the process of preparing for the first North American visit of the sixteenth Karmapa, the head of the Kagyu Tibetan lineage. As I've mentioned, the Karmapa had visited Baba in Gurudev Siddha Peeth, where this Buddhist spiritual leader had spent the night and performed his highly revered Black Crown Ceremony in the ashram's main temple.

The organizer of Baba's talk at Naropa was someone who went by the name Krishna and had met Baba previously. Krishna told me that Naropa was planning for a thousand people to attend. I received a phone message from Baba saying that Naropa should charge six dollars admission for his talk. Krishna was adamant that, in the past, these kinds of talks had always been free. I communicated the situation to Baba, but Baba insisted that there be a charge. This went back and forth a few times, and finally Baba said, "Okay, then charge just one dollar." Krishna finally agreed. The talk was well attended, and at the end of the evening, Baba called Krishna up on the stage. Baba handed Krishna a bag that held all the proceeds of the night, and he said, "I wanted to present you with this donation to help you bring your guru to the United States." Krishna turned bright red when he understood Baba's intention in collecting a fee for his talk. Besides misunderstanding Baba, he had lost out on a few thousand dollars for his cause.

In nearby Denver, where people had seen enough of gurus for the time being, there were not great crowds attending Baba's satsangs. Someone suggested that Baba go to Aspen for the remainder of his Colorado visit. Bruno and I made arrangements for this; we were able to find a house to rent that was suitable for Baba and a few of his staff. John Denver, a well-known singer who had been coming to see Baba, lived in Aspen and one night invited Baba to his house. John had a large telescope and was able to show Baba the planet Jupiter—known as the guru planet—which Baba had mentioned in one of his talks. I wasn't there that evening, but I heard that Baba was really pleased by that.

We began to have chants a few times a day at the house we'd rented for Baba. There were, however, complaints from neighbors about the noise. Baba said we needed to find a place where people could meet that would be suitable for chanting and satsang. Fortunately, a new Community Center had recently been built nearby. Baba suggested we have a one-day event and invite people to join us. He said it would be "intense." We put out the word, and twenty-five to thirty people signed up. I believe we charged thirty-five dollars for the day, just to defray costs. Bruno and I set this up and then stood outside the room, peeking in through the window in the door to see how it was going. Baba saw us and waved us in just in time for meditation. The format was so well received that this format was used later in Aspen for a four-day event that was called the Intensive and it continued throughout the rest of Baba's tour, as well as his next tour, and still continues to this day as the Siddha Yoga Shaktipat Intensive.

*   *   *

From Aspen, Baba moved on to Oklahoma City and then to Chicago and on to Ann Arbor, Michigan, where the first Siddha Yoga ashram in the US had been opened. Baba's tour then continued to New York. After leaving Oklahoma City, a group of us drove across the country to make the arrangements for New York. The New York devotees had found a four-story building on 91st Street on the Upper West Side of Manhattan, one block off of Riverside Drive, that had once been a Russian school. It was perfect for us. Being so close to a path along the Hudson River allowed Baba to have the perfect place to go for a walk, which he loved to do daily. There was a hall large enough to hold six hundred people and many small rooms to house a growing staff.

Lowell Blum had printed a promotion for Baba in a newspaper format called "Meditate," which was full of articles and photos with the dates of Baba's visit on the cover. We distributed hundreds of bundles of these all over the city. We were all excited about Baba's upcoming visit.

This was a giant step for the tour, and we had a big job to do to let the nearly 8 million people who lived in New York City know that Baba was coming. Thousands of small posters were printed with a great headshot of Baba's face. We posted it all over the city. As I knew New York well, I organized a campaign to go out at night and wallpaper the city. Four teams would go out between 10:00 p.m. and 2:00 a.m. and go up and down the city streets to hang these posters everywhere we could. There were many billboards all around the city advertising musical concerts, Broadway shows, and every event imaginable. We always put groups of posters on them. One night a van stopped near us, and the driver leaned out his window and very sternly said, "Hey, you see that poster there? You don't cover that one up." He wasn't asking us; he was telling us. It seemed there were some unwritten rules of billboard advertising that we had to learn.

One night, a group was postering when two policemen were walking nearby. They saw us putting up posters, and one came over to give us a ticket for littering. He said, "What do you have there?" I handed him a poster. He called his partner over, saying, "Hey, look at this." They were both intrigued by the photo. The one policeman kept saying that he had to give us a ticket, but then he would look at Baba's picture and hesitate. He went back and forth a few times, and then he decided to let us go. He said, "Just be careful out there."

This photograph of Baba became known among Siddha Yogis as "the shaktipat photo." So many people told stories about how they'd been walking past that photo and had been drawn to it—and some received shaktipat initiation from it. One man described seeing a face that kept reappearing in his dreams. Then one day when he was walking in New York, he was shocked to see the face from his dreams on a poster—with a name and a phone number. Of course, he came to meet Baba. There were many, many wonderful stories like that.

Baba's New York schedule was incredibly full. There was early morning meditation, the *Shri Guru Gita* recitation, a noon chant, evening satsangs, and meals served for the staff. In the evening satsang, which was always well-attended, Baba would give a talk, followed by a question-and-answer session. As the demand grew, there would be multiple Intensives held during the week. They were split up to accommodate people's busy schedules. One Intensive would be held in the mornings from 8:00 a.m. to noon, Monday through Friday. Then a separate Intensive with different participants was held from 6:00 to 10:00 p.m. In both sets of Intensives, Baba would give talks and would walk around the room during meditation with his wand of peacock feathers giving shaktipat initiation to each person. These morning and afternoon Intensives were held in an upstairs hall five days a week and were always full. Then on the weekends, there would often be a two-day Intensive held all day on Saturday and Sunday. And when he wasn't in Intensives or satsangs, Baba would meet people in small groups in what were called "private darshans." Baba's energy to do all of this was truly amazing to observe.

At this time, the seva I offered was in the hall as a hall monitor. I helped seat people, managed the crowds, answered questions, and was part of the team to clean and prepare the halls. I got up early and by 4:30 a.m., I was lighting incense and preparing the hall for the early morning meditation. I felt blessed to immerse myself in this and to participate in many Intensives in all the major stops over the two and a half years of this tour.

*   *   *

I invited my mother to attend one of the Intensives. She had visited the center at Nandini's a few times before and had enjoyed the satsangs. She sheepishly told me one day that when she walked into the center for the first time and saw Baba's picture, she could have sworn that the picture winked at her. She had by now met Baba on a few occasions. My mother would never come without a small gift of fruit or a small potted plant.

When my mother attended the Intensive, I attended that Intensive as well, as a full participant. During one of the meditation sessions, I sank into a deep state and found myself lifting out of my body and shooting upward through multiple stages and planes until I leveled off someplace where I was in the presence of a group of ten or twelve old men. They were all dressed in black gowns and hats and were standing around me in a semicircle. One among these men appeared much older than the others. He stood at the center of the others. He seemed weak and frail; he was being respectfully supported by one of the other men. I could see that these men saw me as if I were within a globe of bright white light. They seemed exhilarated to see me. I intuited that these were Jewish scholars and ancestors of mine.

After the meditation, during the break, I asked my mother how she was doing. She said that she had gone into a very deep quiet place in herself and saw what she described as a bright blue diamond that sparkled. She later shared this experience with Baba, and he said to her, "Don't lose it this time!" My mother had never read Baba's autobiography, *Play of Consciousness*, and had never heard of Baba's experiences of the Blue Pearl that he describes in his book. During one of the sharing sessions, she said, "I feel like I'm in a room with a bunch of lovely lunatics, but I think it's great."

Years later, I shared with my mother the ancestor experience that I'd had at the same time that she was having her blue diamond experience. She remained intrigued.

Sometime soon after this, my mother was doing some office work in New York City. She was standing near a tall filing cabinet when she suddenly heard chanting of the sort she remembered from the ashram. She later told me that her mind went blank in that moment, and she felt herself being pushed back. The filing cabinet then fell, landing where she had been standing—and coming so close to her that it tore one of her stockings. She was completely unhurt; her leg wasn't even scratched. She told me that she felt protected and that it seemed connected to her ashram experience.

*　　*　　*

One day I was asked to help plan a sightseeing tour of New York City for Baba. He particularly wanted to see what he called the *Mukti Devi*, which translates as "the goddess of liberation." We knew he meant the Statue of Liberty. We made a stop in Battery Park at the foot of Lower Manhattan where there is a clear view of the statue. He commented that Americans use a statue to represent an ideal, just as Indians honor a statue to represent their concept of the Divine.

We also visited the American Museum of Natural History. Baba stopped and was very interested when we passed a life-sized diorama of Native Americans greeting Peter Stuyvesant, who became the first governor of New Amsterdam, later renamed New York. The Native Americans were bare chested, had shaved heads and were wearing only loincloths. Baba commented, "See, Americans used to dress just like Indians!"

When we came into the museum's Great Hall, where there are reconstructed bones of dinosaurs, Baba looked up at the giant Tyrannosaurus Rex and asked me, "Did this one eat people?" I told him that according to our best understanding, the dinosaurs all died out before the rise of humans. He looked at me very seriously and said, "There never was a time when man was not"—a comment I have pondered over many times in the years since.

It was at this time, on Baba's second world tour, that many thousands of people from all over the world were introduced to Baba and his teachings. I loved being there to welcome newcomers almost every day. We were in New York City for quite a few months. We left just before Christmas Day and celebrated Christmas in Atlanta, Georgia, at the home of the Starnes family. Their daughter, Bonnie-Rama, a great devotee and friend, had been with Baba in India.

From Atlanta, we went to Coral Springs, Florida. I had gone ahead with a few others to help prepare a house for Baba and the rapidly growing tour staff. At some point during Baba's stay there, I was asked to drive Damayanti, one of Baba's cooks, to Homestead, Florida, about an hour and a half away, to look for some fresh fruit for Baba. Homestead had enormous tracts of farmland at the time. I remember roadside signs all over saying "Maters and Taters," Southern slang for tomatoes and potatoes. This area is now primarily a rural suburb of Miami. We stopped at a number of farm stands until we found one with lush fruit for sale. Baba wanted tangerines and, because I had lived in Hawaii, I knew how to select the best quality fruit of all types. He was quite pleased with what we bought.

One day in Florida about twenty of us accompanied Baba on a boat ride from a nearby marina. As we were boarding the boat, an old man appeared. He was toothless, shirtless, bald, and seemed to be babbling somewhat incoherently, though he was also quite friendly. Baba commented that it was auspicious before a journey to encounter an *avadhut*, a spiritual being who was free from societal norms. Baba had himself prepared food for us to eat for lunch that day, and he told us to give some of the food he had prepared to this avadhut. The man took the food with great delight; I remember he was laughing. The dish that Baba had made was incredibly delicious. We all enjoyed it later. Baba was a master cook. Every dish he prepared had the indescribable quality of ambrosia. The food he cooked was filled with his energy and with his deep knowledge of Indian spices.

As we continued on the cruise, the captain asked Baba if he would like to take the helm and steer the boat. To our delight he agreed. That morning Baba had given me a maroon colored, felt beret. There is a photo of me standing next to him as he was at the wheel. After some time, we all sat down on the boat benches. Baba closed his eyes, and a powerful energy came over us all. I could feel myself drop into an unusually deep and unusually powerful meditation. This lasted for a while.

When we all came out of meditation, Baba said, "Anyone on this boat will not take birth again." It was a profound experience.

17. THE MAUI TOUR

Baba's next stop was Los Angeles. A group of us drove across the country again to the West Coast to join him. I don't have any memory of our stay there, as within a short time I was sent with Bill Stucky to Maui in Hawaii to prepare for Baba's upcoming visit in about two months. In the early spring of 1975, Bill and I began the task of finding lecture halls, living places for Baba and staff, and all the thousand other things that were required. We stayed with devotees in Pukalani as we did all of this.

Baba had been to Maui in 1974 and stayed at the beautiful Seabury Hall, a private school on the slopes of Haleakala Crater. This school had a panoramic view of the ocean and great accommodations for Baba and his staff. During Baba's time there, he and a small group had gone up to the top of the crater and recited *Shri Guru Gita* at its edge. At that time, Baba had said, "Haleakala is a true sacred place, worthy of pilgrimage."

This year, however, Seabury Hall was not available during Baba's stay. Bill and I scoured the island looking for something suitable where Baba could hold public satsangs. It seemed that nothing like this was available. We communicated this to Baba and were told to keep looking. Finally, after exhaustive searches, we found that Camp Maluhia, a Boy Scout facility on the northeastern side of West Maui was available. This was a much more rustic atmosphere than most of the places Baba had stayed, and it was a much drier region than the lush terrain on the slopes of Haleakala. It did, however, have a large, new, beautiful hall that was perfect for public gatherings. The biggest issue was that camp was much farther for the public to travel. It also required an enormous amount of cleaning and preparation. We painted a room that was to be for Baba, hoping it would be dry before his arrival. This was typical, however, as it seemed that every location we set up around the country came together miraculously at the last moment.

During this time, Bill and I also met with many of the spiritual groups on Maui, and we went to every health food store, public library, and educational institution to put up posters announcing Baba's visit. On one of these excursions to a local library, Bill met Paul Reps, author of *Zen Flesh, Zen Bones*, which was a very well received book and one of the early works on Zen to become popular in the West. The book included many Zen stories and parables, and its final chapter was the author's translation of the *Vijnana Bhairava*, an ancient text that is one of the foundational texts of Kashmir Shaivism. Baba quoted from the *Vijnana Bhairava* many times throughout his teachings, and the text has been studied extensively by Siddha Yoga students. Paul Reps was also a Sanskrit scholar and had studied with Swami Lakshmanjoo, one of the most respected scholars of Kashmir Shaivism.

At the time, I had never heard of Paul Reps, but Bill was familiar with *Zen Flesh, Zen Bones* and arranged for us to meet him at the cottage where he was staying in Kihei. Reps welcomed us warmly and invited us in. After we'd spoken for a few minutes, he asked me, "Why are you so happy?" I was stunned by this question; I hadn't heard it since I was a very young child when everyone, it seemed was asking me the same question. I don't know that I really had an answer for him.

One night Bill and I were staying with some devotees in Kula, which is high up on the slopes of Haleakala at about 3,000 feet above sea level. Bill and I decided to hike into the crater as I had done several times before—but this time it would be by the light of the full moon. At 10,000 feet above sea level, at the crater's edge, the sky is miraculously clear. The mountain's cloud layers usually form at about 8,000 feet. We started walking into the crater itself at about 10:00 p.m. and began to make our way down. The moonlight was so bright that it was like walking under a streetlight. Even though the terrain is unique and the downward slope is persistent, we easily walked for a few hours in that bright, cooling moonlight. At the bottom, we slept a bit and then hiked back up at dawn on the switchback trail, which is a much steeper climb back up the slope.

*   *   *

Finally, it was time for Baba's arrival. As I had been one of the organizers of this leg of the tour, I was able to choose myself as the one to drive Baba from the Kahalui Airport to the retreat site. It was the first time I had driven Baba since we'd been in Pasadena the year before. Driving Baba had always felt natural to me, and I was thrilled to be able to step into this role once again.

As I've mentioned, the retreat site was adequate for the tour's purposes, but it was definitely more rustic and more remote than the tour was used to. People did come to be with Baba, however. One day, Baba called for me and asked me to accompany him on a walk —just the two of us. We walked up the hillside above the retreat site on a quiet path. At one point Baba stopped to look up at Haleakala, which was on the other side of the two volcanoes that make up the island of Maui. I thought he must be remembering his visit to the crater the year before. I felt a bit of remorse that we weren't up there this year.

At one point we stopped by a tree that was full of fruit. "*Neembu?*" Baba asked.

Fortunately, I knew some basic Hindi and knew that this is the word for "lemon." I said, "Yes, Baba," and then he wanted to pick some. I held out the bottom of the shirt I was wearing, and we filled it with lemons. A bit later we passed a jackfruit tree that was full of fruit. This is a large fruit, sometimes eighteen inches or more in length. Baba was pleasantly surprised to see jackfruit, as it grows quite well in India. He said, "We'll send someone back to get some, and I will show the kitchen how it is prepared." We did this and he spent quite a bit of time showing the kitchen staff the unique way to cut and use this unusual fruit. We all shared the delicious result the next day.

On our walk, Baba and I had also passed a patch of gotu kola that was growing on the ground in the shade of another tree. In Hindi it is called *brahmi*. Baba told me, "This herb is very good for the mind and especially for someone who has abused alcohol or drugs, as it has a cooling effect on the brain." In India a hair oil is made from brahmi to use during the hot season. Baba said that a person should eat two gotu kola leaves a day to cool the brain. What a great walk this was, and something I will always remember with great love.

The satsangs on Maui went well despite the fact that people had to travel some distance to get to them. We had a great, energy-filled celebration for *Shivaratri*, which capped off a beautiful visit, and for this people came from all over the island.

Sometime during Baba's visit to Maui, I met someone who suggested a business opportunity for me. As I was running a bit low on funds, I felt the need to pursue this. There was a company, now defunct, called Rhama Products that sold skin cream. This was not anything I could have ever imagined myself doing, but I accepted the challenge. After the tour left, I stayed on Maui for a few weeks to develop this business. I stayed on a communal piece of land known as The Banana Patch. I knew of this property from my first experience on Maui and had actually lived there for a few weeks back then. Now, I stayed with the owner, who had great love for Baba. He asked me to teach him how to chant the *Shri Guru Gita* in lieu of my room and board. We shared a lot during my short stay.

18. OAKLAND, CALIFORNIA, 1975

Now, it was time to return to California. The tour had purchased an old, rundown building in a depressed neighborhood in Oakland and had renovated the property beautifully. This seemed to be Baba's specialty: taking something misused and broken and turning it into something wonderful. This was also indicative of what he did with people all over the world.

This property became the Siddha Yoga Ashram in Oakland, the largest permanent residential ashram on Baba's tour so far. On this property, we had plenty of room to spread out. There was a separate area for Baba's living quarters, many residential rooms for staff, a large kitchen, and a very large hall for public satsangs. The crowds grew.

During this stay, I was again offering seva in the meditation hall. We prepared it early, managed the crowds, vacuumed, and cleaned it —often several times a day. There was an early morning meditation session, a recitation of *Shri Guru Gita*, and public satsangs with Baba in the evening where he would hold question and answer sessions. He also gave numerous special satsangs and Intensives during this stay.

Whenever there was a satsang or special event, I would be on duty just outside the hall to greet the participants. My preference would have been to focus on meditation—to be in the satsang—yet my duties were to stand outside the hall saying hello and goodbye to everyone who came. So, that became my meditation, and I pursued it with enthusiasm. I greeted everyone and answered questions with genuine love. This became a great meditation in itself.

Baba was in Oakland for about ten months. Many, many people met Baba there and received shaktipat, which was the beginning of their spiritual journey. The crowds rapidly expanded. We always had a full house for satsangs and Intensives. Many well-known people came to meet Baba—scientists, astronauts, philosophers, governors, movie stars, popular music artists. . . Gurus and teachers from many different spiritual paths came as well. Baba became known as the "guru's guru."

The *shakti*, the energy, was very strong there, and the Intensives —designed by Baba for spiritual initiation—were unusually powerful. Sometimes during meditation sessions people would display *kriyas*, which were spontaneous movements or sounds that happen as the energy moves through the body. These kriyas help to cleanse the body, mind, and emotions to allow the shakti to flow more freely. Kriyas can also be very subtle, allowing a person's internal experience to deepen and mature. Sometimes people would laugh or cry seemingly spontaneously. This would make for quite a noisy room, especially as Baba would be walking around the room, swatting people with his peacock feather wand and touching them between the eyebrows or on top of their heads. There seemed to be an endless variation of this physical transmission of shakti, but it always produced the deepest and most meaningful experiences for the participants. The other hall monitors and I were always in awe to watch this sacred process unfold. I felt privileged to witness this extraordinary awakening occur in so many people. Every day brought new opportunities to watch the power and intention of Baba's divine mission. I think that everyone who was serving Baba thrived on assisting such a noble cause. Baba's lectures and informal talks were a source of constant inspiration. He was the best storyteller I have ever heard. His wisdom—expressed daily through stories, poetry, and humor—was enthralling.

A reporter once asked him, "Are you God?"

Baba answered, "Yes—and so are you!" Baba's teachings were not only from his own experience but also expressed the exalted experience and writings of saints and mystics of all major spiritual traditions. In various ways, Baba told us again and again that the entire universe is the manifestation of God—that God manifests in and as all creation, including each one of us. That the essence of God is love. That our role is to experience this and to manifest it in every aspect of our daily lives. "See God in each other" seemed to be the official motto of the ashram. I resonated deeply with this understanding as it matched my early experiences, and its continued unfolding in my life.

Baba also had a great sense of humor. One evening after a meditation session ended, while I was on duty outside the door, Baba left the hall, and a few young children followed him out. As the hall doors closed, suddenly Baba passed some gas. The young children began to giggle. Baba looked over in the corner, where there was a stuffed toy frog, and he said, "Hey, that wasn't me! It was the frog!" Baba laughed aloud and ran off like a gleeful schoolboy. The children laughed in delight.

*   *   *

At some point during this period, I was asked to represent Siddha Yoga at a conference organized by the San Francisco Bay Area Interfaith Council. This was a two-day event with representatives from all the faiths, major and minor, in the area. It was an interesting event and there were many perspectives discussed. At lunch time, I happened to share a table with three other people representing Eastern and Asian faiths. There was the abbot of a large Buddhist monastery, a Sufi sheik, a nun from a Hindu order, and myself. Other than me, they were all in their respective traditional dress. The abbot wore a long black robe and had a shaven head. The sheik wore a traditional tan-colored robe and had long hair. The nun wore a traditional white sari. I was in plain Western clothes. We had some interesting discussions which culminated in everyone sharing something of their personal backgrounds. At one point, we discovered that, in fact, we were actually all born Jewish. After a shared moment's look of shocked recognition, the four of us almost fell off our chairs laughing!

During this time, I continued my sales of the Rhama products, and I had some reasonable success with this. It seems odd to think of it now, as it is so very far from any sense of my personal identity and skills. It did, however, provide a very modest side income. At one point I teamed up with a fellow ashramite I'll call Penny. No one would refuse buying this product from Penny as she was the epitome of beauty itself. Some of Penny's friends were well-known people who had been with us on tour in Los Angeles. She and I decided to make a trip there together. I asked Baba's permission to be gone for ten days. He asked who I was taking with me. I told him Penny, and he nodded and said it was fine.

Penny and I were just friends. I had no thoughts of any kind of relationship outside of this sales venture. We borrowed a car, and the ashram kitchen prepared a bag lunch for our six-hour drive. After a few hours we stopped at a rest stop and sat on a grassy area to eat our lunch. Once we had eaten, I felt myself drawn into a meditative state. Like a spell coming over me, I suddenly saw Penny as if she were bathed in a sacred glow. There was light all around her, and I actually heard celestial bells ringing as she spoke. My heart was flung open, as I was irresistibly and obviously in love. I said nothing about this as she and I continued on our drive. We stayed at her mother's house outside of L.A. and then set out to sell our products. We gave facials to two well-known actresses at their homes and also to anyone else we could arrange to meet with. We also visited the home base and laboratory of Rhama Products.

Things were going along fine. Although I hadn't said anything, Penny began to realize that I had strong feelings for her. Unfortunately, she said that she was not at a point in her life where she was ready for a relationship. We talked about this, and I had to accept it—although I felt significantly broken-hearted. I never expected to be in a situation like this. It was all quite a surprise. I had truly only wanted to pursue my spiritual practices. It would seem that Cupid's arrow had penetrated me and not her. I tried my best to contemplate that the love that I felt was within me and wasn't dependent on another person. That, in fact, I was that love.

Penny and I did remain friends, although the mystery of what happened persisted for a very long time. Her laughter, even from a distance, still sounded like music to me. Her voice would penetrate deep into my heart. It took a long time to get over this, and it affected me greatly. I did my best to just let it go.

*   *   *

After we'd been in Los Angeles for about a week, Don Harrison called us to let us know that Baba had just suffered a mild heart attack. We were, of course, stunned by this and planned to return to Oakland right away. Quite concerned, we tearfully headed home. We both were able to visit Baba in the hospital. This was the first time I had ever considered that Baba was vulnerable to physical illness. Up to this point, Baba's strength and vitality had seemed almost unearthly. To see my guru like this was a real eye opener.

After a short stay in the hospital, Baba returned to the ashram in Oakland. He remained in silence while he was recuperating. There was a month-long retreat that had been scheduled to begin in Arcata, California. Baba stayed behind in Oakland for the first two weeks and then joined the retreat. George, who had been in charge of the hall at the ashram, went up to the retreat, and I was left in charge of the hall in the ashram in Oakland. Everything went on as usual. Sometimes Baba would come to the hall in the evenings and sit quietly with us for meditation. It was a serene time, as all the intense activity of the ashram was significantly diminished.

One day, after Baba had left for Arcata, we received a visit from Swami Chidananda Saraswati, who was the current president of the Divine Life Society based in Rishikesh, India. He had succeeded his guru, Swami Sivananda of Rishikesh, after his passing in 1963. Swami Chidananda was a lovely person and was very well respected. He had come to pay his respects to Baba, as he knew that Baba was recuperating. When he learned that Baba was at a retreat in Arcata,

Swami Chidananda asked for a harmonium and, sitting on the floor in front of Baba's chair in the hall, he sang some beautiful *bhajans* and hymns for Baba's health. I was moved by his humility and demeanor.

*   *   *

I still needed to earn some money to be able to continue on the tour, and at one point I had an opportunity to drive a truck for a local health food company. Another ashramite was managing the receiving and delivery of goods from this company's home office in Richmond, California, a few miles north of San Francisco. I would pick up a fully loaded, eighteen-foot refrigerated truck and make deliveries all the way down the coastal highway to Los Angeles. This was a three-day event with two overnights. I was given an extra twenty dollars per night for hotels. Of course, I kept the forty dollars and slept in the truck. The second night I always stayed just outside the Altadena Dairy in the City of Industry, California. The name had seemed odd to me as it was just miles and miles of farmland. On the third day, I would wake up at dawn and try to be the first one in line to pick up cases of yogurt and kefir. The dock man would often offer me an extra bottle or two of kefir for myself. From there, I would make five or six other stops to pick up bread, bakery items, snacks, juices, and frozen goods like ice cream. Once the truck was fully loaded, I would begin the six-hour drive back to Richmond.

The road going home was precarious. Interstate 5 was the fastest route from Los Angeles to San Francisco, but it had a six-mile stretch that was extremely challenging, even dangerous. It was a steep downhill grade all the way. My truck was a manual five-speed unit with a split shift, meaning there were actually ten manual gear positions. I had never driven such a truck and had been given no instructions. That became evident as I careened downhill with no idea how to properly downshift so that I could safely navigate a road like this. I was going much too fast, and this old truck had very bad brakes. Every mile or so, there was a runaway truck exit that ran up a sand filled track to slow a truck down in an emergency. Every time I passed one of these, I considered taking it. My foot would be down to the floor on the brake pedal; I was practically standing on the brake pedal in my attempts to slow down. I always reported the condition of the brakes to the company, but nothing was ever done. I did this once a week for about eight weeks before I quit.

On one of those trips home, I wondered if there was a safer route I could take. What was it like on the side roads? Feeling adventurous that day, I tried another road. That particular side road took me to nothing but open farmland and fields. I went on for several miles, and then the engine suddenly began to sputter. After a few minutes, the truck came to a full stop. The engine was dead, and I was in the middle of nowhere. There was a bar about fifty yards ahead. I walked in and ten men were bellied up to the bar, facing the bartender. I announced that I was a truck driver and had just broken down. I asked whether there was a service station anywhere nearby. It was almost comical as ten heads simultaneously turned around to me and then turned back to what they were doing as if I wasn't there. The bartender then said there was a gas station about ten miles down the road. I wasn't going to get any help here, so I went out to hitchhike. It wasn't more than a few minutes before a station wagon stopped for me. The driver was Basque and spoke with a strong French accent. He had a Collie in the back seat. He was a very kind person, apparently a sheep herder, and he drove me the ten miles to get help. I was lucky that the service station had someone available with a tow truck. After a few hours, I was back on my way. That was the last time I ever veered off the main route.

The next driver to do this job found it so dangerous that he simply parked the truck on the side of the road one day and hitchhiked home, leaving a fully loaded refrigerated truck to its own fate. It's probably what I should have done. A few weeks later I learned that the owner of company was found in his parking lot with a bullet in his head. Apparently, he owed money to the wrong people. I was very happy to be out of there!

19. Back to New York

After about ten months in California, it was time to once more drive back across the country to New York to help prepare for Baba's next visit there. I drove with Peggy Bendet and a man named Harishchandra, in Peggy's Volkswagen Bug. Each of us had relatives in cities along the way, so we decided to stop for a quick hello to each one. My grandfather lived in Phoenix, Arizona; Harishchandra had family in Houston, Texas; and Peggy's parents were in a suburb of Dallas.

I was excited that I would be able to see my grandfather, whom I'd been fond of as a child. Many years had passed since I had seen him. Seeing him was somewhat disappointing, however, as he was then ninety-five, and I wasn't sure he even knew who I was. Still, I was glad that I got to spend some time with him. Each of us had had an opportunity to visit with our respective families before we pushed on into New York.

This was now in September of 1975. I took the last shift at the wheel as I was comfortable driving in New York City. We stayed at an apartment on the Upper West Side of Manhattan in the seventies. A devotee, Rudrani, a local yoga teacher, had an apartment belonging to her father that was available to us. About eight of us were there initially. After a day, some of us headed upstate to prepare the facility Baba was going to stay in, and some of us stayed on in the city to do outreach.

When we first arrived in New York City, I wasn't really tired, and I decided to take a walk in Central Park, which was just a block or so away. Everyone else went to take rest. It was about 7:00 a.m. on a crisp autumn morning. I felt the trees and the quiet of the morning were welcoming me back. I was enjoying being back in New York and wandering through the park was delightful. I was walking along a path heading back toward the apartment when I noticed three people walking on a path that was approaching mine at a forty-five-degree angle. We were walking at about the same speed, and we were going to meet as our paths came together.

As they got closer, I saw there were two men and an Asian woman. I thought one of the men looked like John Lennon, but I wasn't sure because he had shorter hair, and I hadn't seen a recent photo of him. We met at the crossroads, and I stopped and said, "You look like John Lennon. Is that you?" He playfully stepped back a step, looked down at himself and said, with a feigned surprise, in a perfect John Lennon voice, "It probably is!" We both laughed a hearty laugh. Yoko Ono, who was with him, also laughed. We shook hands and as we did, a burst of energy leapt out of me toward him. He noticed this as well, as he reacted with gentle surprise. We wished each other a beautiful day and walked on. When I got back to the apartment, the other people were just having breakfast. When I told them who I had just met they were surprised and a bit disappointed they hadn't decided to walk with me.

As an aside, shortly after his death in 1980, a New York newspaper reported that John Lennon had read an article about the mantra *Om Namah Shivaya* that appeared in the British magazine, *Sight and Sound*. They called it "Swami Muktananda's mantra." According to the New York article, this prompted Lennon to purchase a cassette tape of the chant from the local Siddha Yoga Meditation Center in Manhattan. He had requested and received the cassette a few weeks before he was tragically killed.

*　　*　　*

Shortly after my encounter with John Lennon, I traveled upstate to the DeVille Hotel in South Fallsburg, New York, which the SYDA Foundation had rented for the upcoming six months. It was a beautiful country setting with a large hall that had once been a night club with tiered levels. There were many rooms for people to come for extended stays and plenty of office space for the staff. Baba had a small separate house on the edge of the property. I continued to offer seva in the main hall, managing the seating, cleaning, and preparing the hall for satsangs, and again cleaning afterward. A crew of about five of us shared this responsibility.

The hall would open for early meditation around 4:00 a.m. One of my tasks was to rise at 3:30, shower, and get to the hall to prepare it before people arrived. I would light candles and prepare a puja tray of delightfully fragrant *dhoop*, a unique blend of resins and spices that helped to facilitate a meditative atmosphere. I would offer this tray of burning incense respectfully to Baba's chair and to all the large photos of other siddhas of our tradition that had been hung around the periphery of the room. In the rear of the hall there was a large photo of Baba's own guru, Bhagavan Nityananda. I would then sit for meditation myself. This was a special time, without crowds of people and activity. I always appreciated those moments.

We held many Intensives during this stay. While the Intensives were going on, the hall staff had to be particularly diligent. During the meditation sessions, we had to be alert to Baba's needs as he walked around giving people spiritual initiation. The hall was darkened at these times, and we had to make sure the aisles were clear of obstructions—shawls or handbags or people's feet. Sometimes, too, the participants needed support, and we were ready to assist them as well. The hall staff was supposed to be standing during meditation. However, as Baba came by where I was standing, he would most often swat me on the head with his feathers and motion for me to sit down. Sometimes as I sat, he would tug a tuft of hair on the top of the back of my head at the spot that, to a brahmin, traditionally signifies devotion to God. I felt blessed to be able to participate in the meditation sessions.

*   *   *

That summer, hundreds of people came from New York City and the surrounding areas every weekend to bathe in the ashram atmosphere and partake in the experience of Baba's presence and grace. Many also came from around the world for extended stays. The number of people serving on staff continued to expand as it took a lot of effort for every area to accommodate the growing crowds. The kitchen staff prepared three meals a day. The accommodations staff managed rooms for the staff and guests. The writers wrote and edited books and magazines. The managers managed. The gardeners gardened. The cleaners cleaned. The teaching directors did their work. It was always a beehive of activity. Everyone did their task with great energy and devotion to Baba's mission, which had been defined by Baba as nothing less than a "meditation revolution." These were truly great days!

One day as I was strolling through the main lobby, I saw Baba emerge from a small room that was used for private audiences with him. I stopped for a moment to watch Baba walk by. Malti, who would later become Baba's successor and be known as Gurumayi, was with him as was a young woman I'll call Debra, who also worked in the hall with me. As he passed by, he stopped and sweetly touched my shoulder. As he did so, he said to Debra, "How about him? He's a very good earner." Baba then walked on.

I was stunned. I had been resigned to living the single life, and at this point, marriage was not anywhere on my radar. I believe Debra was as surprised as I was. We were friends and co-workers, nothing more. This, of course, sent me into a bit of a tizzy. Is marriage what Baba wants for me? Is marriage with me what Debra wants? And how was I a good earner when I had almost no money? I was preoccupied with these thoughts for a few days. I would take long walks at night to consider it and pray for guidance. At one point, while Debra was visiting someone in New Jersey, I got to the point where I felt that I should consent and pursue this. I should marry Debra. I tracked her down and called her on the phone. I told her that I thought Baba actually wanted us to get married and that I realized that I wanted it as well. In retrospect, a phone call was probably not the best way to propose. She said, "We'll talk about it when I get home." After considering it for a few days, she decided that she was not ready for such a drastic step.

I then dropped the notion with a certain amount of relief—because in truth, I wasn't ready either. Grateful to have that past me, I continued to offer seva and do my practices.

While we were in South Fallsburg, some of the staff members took the opportunity to work in nearby hotels as waiters and waitresses so that they would be able to continue to remain with Baba. A few of us worked part-time as taxi drivers in the town of South Fallsburg. There were townspeople needing rides to and from their homes, children going back and forth to their summer camps and bungalow colonies, as well as devotees and guests coming from out of town by bus and needing rides to the ashram. It would seem that driving karma was frequently my destiny.

As we waited for passengers at the taxi stand in the town center, the drivers would rotate the calls. Vasudev Levi, who later became Swami Vasudevananda, was also a driver. He often joked that frequently he would get a ride that was going around the corner, and I would get one going ten miles or more, thus earning more of a fare. We certainly couldn't control this, but it did happen a lot.

There were also radio calls for the taxis managed by Mr. Bearman, the owner of Bearman's Taxi. Once I got a call to pick up a rabbi at a certain facility. When I arrived, there was a big send off for this rabbi. As they brought the rabbi to my cab, people were dancing and singing. It was quite festive. One very excited man told me, "You are so lucky to pick up the Grand Rabbi!" The rabbi got into my cab, and as we were driving off, I asked him where he was going. He seemed surprised that I didn't know. I asked whether we should go back to ask, but he said, "No, just drive on. We'll find it." Against my better judgment, we continued. He told me to turn right here, turn left there, go straight here. It wasn't long before it became clear that neither of us knew where we were. At some point he began asking me questions. I shared my background a bit, and we talked about spirituality. Unexpectedly, from his front passenger seat, he grabbed my head and pulled it toward him. I tried hard to still see the road. "Such devotion in someone so young!" he said. "Even if you don't go to synagogue, just eat only matzah on Passover. That would be enough." I thought it was interesting that he was suggesting that I honor my family's Jewish tradition in some small way.

We proceeded to spend an hour or two searching for the bungalow colony that was expecting him. When we finally got there, it was already dark, and it was clear the people there had been worried about where he was. From my perspective, however, it had been a beautiful opportunity for me to spend time with this respected man.

PART FOUR—DEDICATION

20. The Courtyard Days, 1976–78

We all knew that this second world tour was coming to an end. Baba was planning to return to the ashram in India very soon. One of the staff members came to me one day and said that he had been asked to put together a work crew to go ahead to India to help make preparations in the ashram there. He had never been to India and couldn't find anyone who would agree to go. Amma suggested he speak to me because I had lived there for some time. As I described the ashram's atmosphere and my experiences there, we were quickly able to muster a group of twelve men who were eager to get on board. They left within a few weeks.

By September of 1976, Baba left for the European leg of that tour. Some of us stayed on for a week to help close up the DeVille. Malti also stayed for a few days. As we were cleaning, she came to the hall with Damayanti, holding a pair of Baba's shoes that had been left in Baba's closet. The guru's feet are given a high degree of respect in India, and therefore the guru's shoes or sandals are as well. "Who is worthy of these?" Malti asked. Damayanti pointed to me, and I was the grateful recipient. I still have them in my meditation room today.

Baba traveled on through Europe, visiting England, Germany, Switzerland, and France before returning to India in October of 1976. I followed as soon as I could. Groups of people were flying regularly by jumbo jet, eager to continue their Siddha Yoga experience in Ganeshpuri. Gurudev Siddha Peeth swelled with activity. A new dormitory building, called Mukteshwari, had been built in Baba's absence to house the growing number of devotees. In addition, other dorms and offices were built above a newly covered courtyard, as well as an Amrit building to provide snacks and comfort food for those preferring Western diets. A new medical center had also been built to support the health needs of the ashramites. It was a far cry from the austerity of the early days.

I was asked to manage the main courtyard where Baba gave satsang and darshan each day. This was often challenging as many of the new arrivals had never traveled in Asia before, and India was a totally new experience for them. It would take a while for them to begin to understand the culture and the ways of living in the ashram. Wanting to be with Baba and to deepen their spiritual practices allowed them to adapt. Most did very well.

In the upper garden, a new hall had been built as a second story to Turiya Mandir. The first Intensive after we returned was to be held there. As my duty was in the main courtyard, I wasn't able to participate in the Intensive. I was asked to help with the seating and then return to the courtyard. I had participated in many of the Intensives on the second world tour, and I felt the loss of that privilege now. I asked Swami Premananda, a long-time Baba disciple who was responsible for the overall management of the main temple and courtyard, if I could at least attend the Intensive during Baba's talk. He agreed, and I found a spot on the outside back steps where I would be able to hear Baba's voice. I felt a bit odd doing this as I was essentially sitting behind Baba's chair, separated from him by a wall. At some point in his talk Baba said, "The guru knows all his disciple's needs. He knows even if he has grown a beard." I don't know who else Baba may have been referring to, but I had recently grown a beard, and I knew I really shouldn't have been sitting where I was. At that point I left. From then on, I focused only on my duties in the courtyard.

*   *   *

The seva I offered was all-consuming. I was in the courtyard from 4:00 a.m. until 10:00 p.m. seven days a week with only a twenty-minute break for lunch.

I had to be there, as Baba could appear at any time, and I had to manage the crowds that would form. If I ran to the bathroom and returned to find Baba sitting out, he would say, "Where were you?" in a stern voice. "Bathroom, Baba," I would reply. He would say, "Bathroom *tik hai,*" meaning the bathroom was okay. It was clear that I was expected to be there. When Baba would go back inside, I cleaned the courtyard. There was constant sweeping as leaves were always falling. Everything had to be spotless. If a leaf fell, it had to be picked up, regardless of what else was going on, even during satsangs. In the early morning, I had to make sure the courtyard was clean before *Shri Guru Gita* recitation began. I must have swept that courtyard ten or more times a day.

One of my fondest memories is of watching Baba in the Nityananda Temple in the early morning. The Temple was still being expanded. Before the statue of Bhagavan Nityananda was installed in 1971, there had been a life-sized photograph of Bhagavan in a wooden frame that rested against the south wall. (This photo was later moved to the main dining room.) I tried to be present in or near the temple in the early morning when Baba would come after his bath, well before anyone else was around. He would be freshly dressed in a knee-length piece of cloth tied around his chest. His forehead was smeared with sacred ash. Sometimes I would silently observe from the temple window. Baba would look at his guru's picture for a moment, then prostrate himself, fully outstretched on the floor. Even after reaching such an elevated state, he was still so humble before his guru. Witnessing the depth of his devotion was extremely powerful for me.

I found myself wanting to sit and soak up the rarified atmosphere of the ashram, yet I was kept busy all day long. I remember saying to myself, "Okay, if you want to meditate, you had better do it now with your eyes open as you attend to your duties." This became my sadhana. This pattern had been repeating since the day I met him. Sometimes as I swept the courtyard with the coconut-frond broom, I would be filled with a soft blue light. The entire world would become this light. The ground itself felt soft and alive, as if I were sweeping Baba's body. Sometimes I would be in ecstasy as I swept. Each sweep of the broom was magical. I was very happy. On the rare occasion when I could sit and close my eyes for a moment, I would sometimes sink very deep into a beautiful space.

*   *   *

I often had to explain to newcomers the "what" and "why" of how things were done in the ashram. One day, Baba saw me doing this, and he called me over. He said, "You don't have to talk so nicely to everyone. Just tell them to follow the ashram discipline or go home." Some people may have resented my role as occasional disciplinarian, but I knew that following the ashram discipline was the best way for them to absorb what was being given to them. Still, I did try to do this as nicely as I was able.

There used to be a life-size statue of Bhagavan Nityananda standing in the main courtyard, not far from Baba's seat. This statue had been made by Mahadev Siegel, one of Baba's American students, in the early 1970s. The statue depicted Bhagavan standing with his right arm and index finger raised. The statue's base was in the shape of a pink lotus, surrounded by a scalloped pool, six feet or so in diameter. The pool was tiled all around; it could hold water but was rarely used as a fountain. (It was later moved back to make more room close to Baba's seat.)

Cleaning this statue and its base was part of the seva I offered. When people arrived in the ashram, they would bring all sorts of gifts to Baba. Frequently, he would give these gifts to me to place around the sides of the fountain. There were so many things that I began to group them into little arrangements: two elephants facing a crystal egg, swans emerging from a small *Nataraj*, and so on. There may have been twenty or so little arrangements at any given time. Cleaning this became an additional chore. Everything had to look perfect, as Baba would sometimes notice it as he walked by.

One day someone gave Baba two candles in a crystal base, and he gave them to me for the fountain display. When walking by later he said to me, "Don't be an American candle." I had no idea what he was talking about. It seemed like a strange random comment. I was thinking about it all morning. When I went to clean later that afternoon in the heat of the day, I saw that the candles were leaning and bending significantly in India's heat. When I picked these candles up, I saw that each of them had a label underneath that said, "Made in the USA." I got the message. "Don't melt in the pressure of the moment. Be strong."

Once there was a German man who came to stay for a few days. He was very unruly. He seemed angry at everything. One morning he came to the courtyard for the *Shri Guru Gita* recitation with a large stick in his hand. He kept the stick with him as he sat down. I wasn't comfortable with this and asked him to please put the stick away. He immediately jumped up and began cursing at me in German. "*Schwein! Hund!*" He yelled loudly and threateningly, and I knew the words meant "pig" and "dog" in German. He then raised his stick as if to attack me. I respectfully folded my hands in front of him and said calmly, "You have to give me the stick." He instantly calmed down, handed the stick to me, and sat down for the rest of the chant. I always felt totally protected and never felt an instant of fear.

*   *   *

When Baba was sitting out, I would stand at the back of the courtyard. There were many times during the day when he would be out and no one else was around. If Westerners appeared to pursue their favorite hobby, which was Baba watching, I was to tell them to move on and continue their work. That left many times each day when it was just Baba and me in the courtyard. Sometimes he would be reading, sometimes just sitting quietly. He would sometimes appear to be writing or drawing something with his index finger. He would be writing on his thigh or on his cushion. He seemed focused as he did this, as if he were actually making something happen. I often wondered what it was.

Sometimes a group of visitors would arrive, and Baba would allow them to come for darshan and then invite them to tour the gardens. Some of the Indian boys would be on duty to show them around. Babu Rao Pahelwan, one of Baba's oldest disciples, would also lead tours. Babu Rao and I became good friends. He was quite elderly but had the stamina of a young man. He was always busy doing something. He would play the harmonium for the evening chants, and occasionally, in celebrations, he would dance during the chants, wearing bells on his ankles. He did this with such great delight.

These hours and days in the courtyard were very precious. Just watching Baba interact with people was an education in itself. He portrayed such attention and compassion. He seemed to give each person precisely what they needed. I felt privileged to witness it all. I loved the atmosphere in the courtyard. Whether or not there were crowds present, the dappled light that filtered through the mango trees shading the courtyard always seemed to highlight the peace that pervaded every inch of this sublime space.

Baba's reputation for practical and spiritual wisdom was widely known, and famous people from across the entire spectrum of Indian society would come to see him. State and central government ministers and politicians from all levels of Indian government were frequent visitors. This included the president of India, the vice president, and many state governors. Well-known scholars, actors, and artists of all stripes came. I particularly enjoyed seeing people of many different faiths coming to experience Baba's presence. There was a mother superior from a convent in Bombay who was very fond of Baba and used to bring groups of nuns to have his darshan. There were Hindus, Muslims, Jains, Christians, and Jews—all of whom seemed to recognize Baba's universal teaching of unity. I was inspired by this in particular, as it matched my personality and my background of desiring world peace and integration of all people and religions. Baba's essential teaching seemed to resonate with everyone:

Honor your Self, worship your Self, meditate on your Self. God dwells within you as you.[4]

*   *   *

Just before Christmas in 1976, after the evening chant, Shyama Amma, who was a master of decorating things, and another Indian woman and I were putting up all kinds of Christmas-like ornaments in the mango trees of the courtyard. We had put cotton on some of the branches to look like snow. There was an inflated Santa Claus figure in the tree. It was already dark and no one else was around. Baba came out of his house and called me over. He asked, "So, who is this Santa Claus?" To the best of my ability, I told Baba that Santa was a saint from an area that is now Turkey who loved to give gifts to children on the day that celebrates the birth of Jesus. When I said the word "saint," Baba lit up, "He was a saint!" he said with eyes open wide. Baba was very interested. I then added, "And every year on Christmas Eve, Santa flies on a sleigh pulled by eight reindeer and comes down people's chimneys to bring gifts." Baba looked at me with great seriousness, as if he wasn't sure whether I believed this or not. To not shatter my belief, he gently said, "It is entirely possible." And then he went inside. A few minutes later, he emerged wearing a Santa Claus hat and giant sunglasses. He said, "Santa came early!" and passed out cookies to us. We all laughed and thoroughly enjoyed this precious moment.

Sometimes Baba could be quite stern as well, according to the needs of the moment. One day, a man from South Africa came to visit for the day. He had been attending a conference on vegetarianism in Bombay. While having darshan with Baba, he asked a few questions. Baba spoke quite directly to him. "How can you be so concerned with vegetarianism when you eat people! Your system of Apartheid causes great harm. That is worse than eating meat." Baba was against any form of discrimination by caste, creed, or religion.

---

[4] Swami Muktananda's essential teaching is reprinted from "Essential Siddha Yoga Teachings," https://www.siddhayoga.org/teachings/essential

One day a man came into the courtyard while Baba was sitting out. There was something strange about this man. Outwardly, he looked quite ordinary, but I saw that there was an aura of something very wrong about him, something dark. This man sat quietly for a while, and then he got up and started walking toward the back of the courtyard as if he were going to the lower gardens. I stopped him and politely requested that he sit back down and wait a few minutes. I told him that very soon someone would come to give a tour of the gardens. He sat for a moment or two and then stood up to head for the back. Again, I calmly asked him to sit and wait. My Hindi is minimal but adequate for that situation. This went on a few more times before Baba took charge.

Baba got up and began yelling at this man and hitting him with a bamboo stick he had in his hand. Baba said, "What, you don't listen to my student!" He then chased the man across the courtyard and out the front gate into the street, hitting him all the way. Baba gave instructions to the guards at the front gate to not let this man back into the ashram. Baba then came back into the courtyard and said to me, speaking so sweetly, "Now, he'll listen to you."

A few hours passed, and this same man returned. He calmly walked right past the front guards and into the courtyard. The guards didn't recognize him because he looked totally different. His overall demeanor was light, almost angelic. He literally glowed. I knew it was him, and I looked to Baba to see if I should intervene. Baba would often give me an unspoken signal as to how he wanted me to handle a situation. When he saw the man, Baba just smiled. The man walked right up to Baba, bowed deeply before him, and then he left. The transformation was truly extraordinary. I wondered what karmas, what negativities, he had been relieved of by Baba's actions.

*　　*　　*

Baba often gave me very specific instructions as to how to care for the various plants and trees that adorned the courtyard. Everything was watered by hand, using buckets, which we filled with a water spigot at the back of the courtyard. "That tree gets two buckets of water once a day, this one gets one bucket," he would say. In the hot season, I was to water twice a day. Baba would notice if a tree looked like it needed more water, and he would instruct me. He had studied horticulture when he was younger, along with cooking, astrology, Ayurvedic medicine, and other sciences. It seemed as if Baba knew so much about so many things. He had even studied sword fighting as a young man. He said he gave it up after a bad wound to his wrist, and he showed us his scar.

One day, the courtyard was full of devotees during a quiet darshan time. I suddenly heard the rustle of a coconut tree frond in the tree under which people were sitting. These fronds are about eight feet long, very heavy and could easily hurt anyone sitting below. As the frond began to fall, Baba called out loudly, "Ra-a-am!" As he said this, the coconut frond shifted its angle so that its heavy base faced downward and landed standing up in the dirt that surrounded the tree. This was very different from the way it would normally have fallen. No one was hurt. We simply carried the frond away, and the stillness of the moment returned.

Day in and day out, as it had been on tour, I would drink in the constant and fascinating events and interactions that unfolded around me.

Something that was always fun was when Baba's elephant—whom he called Swami Vijayananda or just Viju for short—came into the courtyard. Every day at 3:00 p.m., Viju would arrive, often trumpeting with delight as he approached the courtyard and heard Baba's voice. The ashramites would all gather to watch this great spectacle. Viju would lower his head and front legs as if to bow and then place a sandalwood garland around Baba's neck. Baba would then feed the elephant bundles of sugarcane and bunches of bananas, followed by all kinds of Indian sweets. Sometimes there would be chocolates that had been brought as gifts for Baba.

All the Westerners would salivate at this, as good chocolates were rare for those of us who had been living in the ashram for a while. Once someone brought a bag of good quality Godiva chocolates that were meant as a gift for Baba. After the crowds left the courtyard, we found the bag sitting in a corner, apparently forgotten. I have to confess that Mr. Varma, who worked in the courtyard with me when he visited, and I sat down and ate quite a bit of the chocolate in that bag. Mr. Varma was an elderly Indian farmer who regularly brought the bananas and sugarcane for Viju. He and I had become good friends over time and although his English was minimal, we shared a lot of heartfelt moments.

Before Viju left the courtyard, Baba would smear some of the finest heena oil all over the elephant's body. The scent would be intoxicating. Viju would then leave with his trainers, but almost never before he had left a huge dung pile on the courtyard marble. Although his trainers would arrive with a buckets and shovels to carry the dung out with them, the floor still required plenty of cleaning and scrubbing afterward by me and, when I had one, an assistant.

Nowadays, people will often ask me to tell them a Baba story from this time. But really, we had a life with Baba, not just a series of stories. I loved every minute of it. I thrived on the whole atmosphere.

And all the while, I was being transformed from within.

21. Sannyasa Initiation, 1977

I was fully committed to the idea that this was my life. I wanted nothing more than to serve Baba and his stated mission of creating a "meditation revolution"—a worldwide transformation in which people would remember their true nature and, therefore, divine love and peace would flow throughout all of humanity. In 1977, Baba had announced that he would be initiating a few Westerners into an ancient order of *sannyasa*, which is monkhood. In April of 1977, two days prior to the beginning of the actual ceremonies, I was approached and asked whether I would accept sannyasa initiation if I were offered the opportunity. I readily agreed and my name was added to the list.

This group of about-to-be initiates consisted of seven Westerners and seven Indians. Baba had given this initiation once before in the late '60s to a few Indian men but never before to Westerners.

The two-day sannyasa ceremonies were quite specific and extensive, all according to ancient rites and rituals that are drawn from to the eighth-century teachings of Adi Shankaracharya. Baba had brought Mahamandaleshwar Swami Brahmananda, who was the current head of the Jyotir Math in North India, to oversee the ceremonies, which added to their authority.

*   *   *

The ceremonies began with a ritual to initiate the participants into the stage of *brahmacharya*, "studentship," which traditionally precedes sannyasa initiation. During this initial process, our heads were shaved. This was followed by a fire ritual, where we performed our own funeral rites to symbolize our dying to our former life and our becoming free from all past impressions. This went on for hours. We then sat up for the rest of the night, silently reciting special mantras and meditating. Just before dawn, we immersed ourselves in the nearby river, throwing away the clothes we were wearing, while certain mantras were recited to symbolize a new birth.

I will never forget the beauty of that moment. It was still dark outside. The sky was completely clear and filled with stars. We were facing east as we entered the river. The planet Venus, which is the morning star, was enormous and bright. We were then asked to take seven steps toward the north, symbolizing a journey toward the Himalayas where we would turn our backs on the pulls and attractions of the world. Then, very loudly, it was called out, "Wait, the world needs you! You must come back for the good of humanity." We returned to the shore and were given the traditional orange robes to wear. At this point, I felt totally cleansed and new, like a newborn child.

We then gathered to get our new monastic names. I was given the name Swami Sadananda Saraswati. *Sada* means "always" or "ever," and *ananda* means "spiritual bliss." Amma told me that Baba specifically asked that I be given this name. We all had the title Swami, indicating monkhood, and the identifier *Saraswati* as that was the branch of sannyasa to which we now belonged. The fourteen of us then met with Baba, who performed the final initiation. Baba covered his head and ours with a white cloth, and he then whispered a sacred mantra into our ear. One by one, we came up to Baba for that special moment. I felt that I had crossed a new threshold that was completely in sync with my deepest inner being and my life's purpose.

The following morning as we prepared for the *Shri Guru Gita* recitation, Baba said there should be a separate section up front for the swamis and that a blanket should be spread for them to sit on. My duties were still in the courtyard, so this task fell to me. I took my usual spot at the back of the courtyard. During the day, I continued my duties in the courtyard as before.

A few days later, all the new swamis were directed to attend classes that were being taught by Swami Tejomayananda. They were taught the reading of Sanskrit texts like the *Rudram* and others. They learned to read these in the original Sanskrit alphabet, Devanagari. I had never learned to read Devanagari, and it intrigued me. I asked Baba if I should attend. His response was very loving, "No, you don't need that. Your duties are here." I just continued on with my regular schedule, but I did feel some envy as the other new swamis were meeting regularly, and I couldn't be there. However, my days were spent close to Baba in the courtyard, and I was quite content with that.

A few more days passed, and I was approached by Swami Prakashananda, an elder swami who visited regularly from his Saptashringi Ashram near Nashik. He had been an early disciple of Baba's and was generally regarded as having a very high attainment. In 1970, I used to clean the room that was kept for him in Turiya Mandir in the upper gardens. Swamiji approached me and said, "Now you are a swami so you should find another seva. You shouldn't be sweeping the floors." I listened respectfully and later asked Baba if that's what I should do. He was quite clear in his response. "Just continue your seva here. Everything is fine."

Later that day I saw Swami Prakashananda coming out from Baba's house. He came over to me somewhat upset. He said, "I never told you not to do your seva. We are all here to serve Baba. I never told you that." He hesitated and then said, "But just don't do the mopping of the floors, everything else is okay." I kept silent. He was referring to the cleaning of the floors after the elephant left the courtyard. I just kept doing my regular duties, whatever they might be, as I felt I had Baba's support to do that.

*   *   *

I loved being a swami. It felt like the most natural role for me. My days were still spent in the courtyard from 4:00 a.m. until 10:00 p.m., and I felt like I was doing what I was supposed to be doing. I did, however, at times feel a bit left out, as I watched some of the other new swamis take on more teaching roles. I was the courtyard swami. Manage the crowds. Keep everything clean. Attend to Baba's needs.

Sometimes I was out of the loop of communication. One afternoon I saw all of the swamis emerge from Baba's house. They must have gone in from the back side as I hadn't seen them enter. As they came out, I approached one of the swamis and asked what was going on. He said that there had been a special meeting with Baba.

"Where were you?" he asked in his unique Southern drawl.

"No one told me anything about it," I said.

"Well," he replied, "you just have to keep your ears to the ground." I asked what Baba had said.

"A lot of things," he went on.

"Just tell me one thing!" I persisted.

He then said that Baba had advised them, "Don't think you have become a swami. You should think you have become the Self." These words lit me up as if I had been there. I felt I had gotten the essence of the meeting. I thanked him for sharing that. In that one moment, I realized that being a swami was just another role to play in this world. I let that understanding sink deep within me. I felt Baba had freed me from identifying myself with the "role" of being a swami.

I immersed myself in my duties. Still having no time for formal meditation, I again focused my mind on open-eyed meditation. My experiences went deeper. I began to see that everything I was experiencing outside myself was actually happening within me. All the sensations of sight, sound, smell, feel, and taste were being interpreted by my mind. I began to see inside and outside of me as one and the same. I would be immersed in a state that was divine. My true being was at the root of it all. I was not my mind or the sensations I perceived. I was not even the witness to them. My true nature was luminous and transcendent. Yet everything was also real. The world itself was truly the infinite body of God, and I was that essence.

When I looked at Baba, I would feel that he was inside me and also outside at the same time. I remember once saying to myself, "How fortunate I am to be able to know the inner Guru and the outer Guru as one and the same. And to see them at the same time." I felt blessed. I remember once looking at Baba from the back of the courtyard and thinking, "I won't always have this ability to see him with my physical eyes." I remember saying to myself, "Oh, my eyes, remember this moment. Drink in this vision. Never forget this." To this day, when I think of Baba, I see him sitting there in the courtyard on his seat, and I am taken back to that moment with great joy.

The courtyard was full of magic. Such a sacred place. One day I was there alone after cleaning. Quite suddenly, with my eyes open, I saw a powerful sphere of bright light, perhaps two feet in diameter, enter the courtyard and swirl around and around rapidly before disappearing. Was this a being of light come to visit? Truly the ashram was a sacred land of gurus, siddhas, and saints.

I continued my contemplations like this, offering every second of every moment to the understanding of the unity of God, Guru, and Self. My every breath was an offering. Everything that I perceived was in that stillness. One day in a moment like this, I quietly passed some gas without losing that state. It was just part of the moment. I didn't think anything of it at the time.

A week or so later, during a large satsang in the courtyard, Baba was talking about remembrance of God. He pointed to me and said, "Look at this swami. He thinks of God all the time. Even when he passes wind, he's thinking of God." Everyone laughed, including Baba. For days afterward people would ask me, "Are you thinking of God now?" with a laugh.

The early morning *Shri Guru Gita* recitation was held in the courtyard during good weather. I was responsible for seating everyone. Sometimes I would then take a seat on the lower part of the platform near Baba's seat. It so happened that being quite tired from the early hour, I would often fall asleep after the first few verses. As much as I tried, my eyes would just close. Malti would be sitting in the front row, just below me. One morning as I nodded off, she took a single peacock feather and, holding it behind her back, tickled my nose with it to wake me up. The women around her noticed and giggled. I sat up straight but nodded off again. She then had Jani, who was probably five or six years old and who sat right next to Malti, do the job. I was mildly embarrassed, but we were all having fun.

I was generally happy while pursuing my practices. Tired but happy. One day in the courtyard Baba was giving a talk about contentment. He pointed at me and said, "Look at him. He's always smiling." Of course, I then had a smile that was probably ear to ear. Baba laughed as did the crowd. Now, I was even happier. I had grown close with the Indian swamis who worked in the main temple, Baba sometimes referred to me as his "American Indian Swami."

*   *   *

One day early in May of 1977, I was standing near Baba in the courtyard when no one else was around. We both looked up as we heard a large group of crows circling and cawing very excitedly just outside the northeast corner of the courtyard. In India this is considered to be an ominous sign. With a face of concern Baba said, "*Bahut kharab*" meaning "very bad." He went inside after a few minutes. A few days later, Baba suffered a severe heart attack. He spent the next few months recuperating.

During this time, he was visited by Muppinarya Swami, the chief disciple of Siddharudha Swami. Siddharudha Swami had given Baba sannyasa many years before and had also given him his monastic name, Swami Muktananda. Muppinarya Swami had taught Baba Vedanta at Siddharudha's ashram. Muppinarya Swami and Baba had not seen each other for many years. I felt honored when Amma introduced me to him in the courtyard as being one of Baba's American swamis. I felt I was connecting to Baba's life history.

Muppinarya Swami was a beautiful being. There is a very moving video of their meeting in Baba's house.

The annual monsoon began within a few weeks of this. This meant heavy rains, sometimes for days at a time. The monsoon season would typically occur from mid-June until mid-September. As there were no darshan times and all the chants were being held inside the main temple, I spent my days sweeping and clearing the mud that would result from the heavy rains. We spread large rolls of burlap material covering pathways through the courtyard, as the marble floors became quite slippery when they were wet. Shripati Lynn had the idea to build a two-feet wide rubber squeegee, which was a great help in cleaning. During these months, I would still spend my normal schedule from 4:00 a.m. to 10:00 p.m. in the courtyard. When I wasn't cleaning, I would sit under the overhang by Baba's seat, watching the rain and reading. It was a quiet time during which I read the entire four-volume *Shiva Purana*, an extensive text that describes the mythology of Shiva and other deities and that may date back between five hundred to a thousand years. It is a great philosophical text in which the stories represent the play of subtle spiritual energies.

At some point toward the end of monsoon, I received a message from Baba that there was too much noise in the courtyard and that I should keep everyone quiet. I would frequently have to convey this message to people who were talking loudly. One weekend, an ashram trustee arrived and was generously, yet boisterously, inviting everyone to the Amrit for snacks as his treat. I went over to him and quietly conveyed Baba's message. This respected man was a bit upset about what I said and perhaps saw it as an insult. It did not ingratiate me with several of the trustees; however, I was just doing my duty at the time.

*   *   *

As Baba began to recover, he started coming out to the courtyard a bit. One morning in September 1977, he arrived in the courtyard with a broom in his hand. A few of the trustees who had come from Bombay for the weekend were present. Baba shouted, "Everyone grab a broom!" And he began sweeping. He moved along sweeping his way down to the lower gardens, yelling all the time. "Where are the princesses? Everyone should sweep! The trustees as well. From now on every Saturday for two hours, everyone will clean. Everything should be clean, inside and outside. You should pick up a broom and sweep your heart."

Everyone was sweeping the pathways and the gardens. I was overjoyed at this, as suddenly everyone was sweeping along with me. After twenty minutes or so, Baba returned to his seat in the courtyard and said, "Ah, now we have built the ladder to heaven!" It was great to see him so animated again. And life went on like this. Every day was a new adventure. Baba had returned to many of his usual routines.

Baba rarely spoke to me other than to give an instruction. Sometimes, however, he would just say something to me as he walked past. One otherwise ordinary day as he walked by, he said, "It is much harder to become a householder after sannyasa than the other way around." At the time it had no context, and it therefore made no sense. I pondered it for some time.

A few months later, unbeknownst to me, there was a wedding scheduled in Bombay for Rani Shetty, a close devotee. The wedding party was coming to the ashram for Baba's darshan immediately after the ceremony. This was on a full moon day when, according to tradition, swamis were to shave their heads. We normally had to do this before noon. Being a bit late due to courtyard duties, I scooted out right after lunch to the small local barbershop just outside the ashram gate.

When I got back to the ashram, I was bare chested, holding my shirt, and planning to run to my room for a quick shower. To my surprise and shock, Baba was in the courtyard with the wedding party. He immediately called me to him. "Where were you?" he said sternly. I tried to answer but it was no use. He kept asking. "Where were you? Why did you leave?" He then said a few things in Hindi that I didn't understand. Afterward, I asked an Indian devotee what Baba had said that wasn't translated. Reluctantly the devotee answered, "He said things that shouldn't be asked of a swami." I pressed him further and he said, "Baba was saying, 'Did you think it was your wedding?'" I was a bit taken aback but let it be. For the next few days, every time Baba saw me, he kept asking, "Why did you leave?" I tried to explain that I wasn't told about the wedding, or I would have been there, but it didn't help much. I had to just let it go and continue my duties.

*   *   *

In early 1978, we went on a *yatra* with Baba to some of the sacred places in Maharashtra state. First, we went to Alandi, where there is a shrine to Jnaneshwar Maharaj, a thirteenth-century poet-saint who is revered for his commentary on the *Bhagavad Gita*. Jnaneshwar wrote in the Marathi language, making the teachings of this Sanskrit scripture available to the local population for the first time. Jnaneshwar is said to have been sixteen when he wrote that text, *Jnaneshwari*, which is still widely read today. We also went to the village of Dehu, where Tukaram Maharaj, another great Maharashtrian saint, lived and sang his abhangas, his devotional poems. In addition, we stopped in Nashik, where we were able to visit many shrines and temples on the banks of the holy Godavari River.

Three of us who were on this yatra—myself, Indu Kline, and Peter "Passport" (who was then in charge of the ashram's passport office)—took a side trip to Trimbakeshwar, about twenty miles from Nashik. The *Shiva Purana*, which I had just read during the monsoon season, described the twelve major *svayambhu*, or "self-manifested," *shiva-lingams* in India. One of these was at the Trimbakeshwar Shiva Temple, and I had a great interest in seeing it. We entered the main shrine as a special puja was just beginning in the inner sanctum, which was on a deeper level down a few steps from the main temple room. There was a silver lingam dome there, perhaps eighteen inches high, and around this was a group of Brahmins who began chanting. These pujas had been performed regularly here since ancient times. During the puja, the Brahmins removed the dome revealing three smaller lingams of stone. The energy from these was so strong that I could visibly see three streams of energy coming off of the top of them, like fountains of the Ganges. Amazing energy.

The samadhi shrine of Jnaneshwar's older brother and guru, Nivrittinath, was also there on a nearby hill, and I was very drawn to see this. It has been said that the two brothers both took live samadhi in the thirteenth century. What this means is that they were alive as they entered their tombs and have remained there, alive and conscious, ever since. Jnaneshwar was twenty-two years old at his entombment, and Nivrittinath was twenty-four. Their ages differ in some accounts.

There had been many flower sellers in front of the Trimbakeshwar temple, and I assumed that there would also be some by Nivrittinath's shrine as well, so we began walking up the hill for ten minutes or so. When we arrived, however, there were no flower shops or people around. I remembered the verse from the *Bhagavad Gita* that said offering a leaf or some water was precious to the Lord. There was a mango tree beside the samadhi shrine, and so we picked a few leaves for an offering and entered what was then only a small structure, perhaps forty by fifty feet in dimension. The shrine and tomb were at the far end.

As soon as I walked into the shrine, I went into what I can only describe as a timeless state and quite unexpectedly saw Nivrittinath himself sitting there. Uncontrollably, my body ran to him. I fell on top of the simple stone tomb and began having intense trembling movements—*kriyas*—while laying over the top. Nivrittinath then spoke to me in Marathi, saying, "Oh my brother, you have come!" I don't speak Marathi, but I understood every word he said. At that moment, the caretakers of the shrine, an elderly man and his wife, ran to me with great concern but apparently, as they saw my state, they must have felt it was okay, as they let me be. The kriyas subsided in a few minutes, and I returned to my normal state, amazed that I had done this. My nature would usually be very pious and respectful in this situation. To me, it seems entirely true that Nivrittinath is still there and is very much alive. This is a precious memory. I have seen in recent photos that the shrine itself has since been renovated and expanded considerably.

22. HONOLULU BOUND

1978: Here, I am sitting with Baba at the Kaimuki Elementary School in Honolulu just after an evening satsang at the beginning of Baba's third world tour.

In June of 1978, Baba came out to the courtyard one early afternoon. He looked very excited. With a big smile, he said to me, "We are going out on tour again, and we are sending you to Honolulu to prepare for my visit. You can make your arrangements." I did so and prepared to leave.

I didn't want to leave Ganeshpuri, but I loved Hawaii and was excited for a new phase of development. At the time there were three Siddha Yoga meditation centers on the island of Oahu, as well as one on Maui and one on Kauai. When the day came for me to leave, Baba told me that I was to close all three centers on Oahu and that they should become one. He said, "Wherever you are, that is the center. You can visit the Maui and Kauai centers when you can. You should write to me every ten days to let me know how things are going." He gave me his blessings and then had Pratap Yande, whom we called Dada, take me to the main temple to circumambulate the murti of Bhagavan Nityananda. And, with that, I was off.

After stopping for a layover of a few hours at the airport in Narita, Japan, I arrived in Honolulu. I was greeted by a group of Baba's devotees with the welcoming spirit of aloha, and then I was taken to the home of a person who had generously agreed to host me until other arrangements could be made. There, too, a crowd of devotees was waiting to welcome me. In the traditional Hawaiian manner, I was garlanded with many leis of the most fragrant flowers. I felt quite welcomed.

After a week or so, I was joined by Kubera Monson, who was in charge of the SYDA Foundation property acquisitions for Baba's tour. Kubera was to help locate properties suitable for Baba's public lectures and programs. Kubera and I both stayed at the Nuuanu home of Lakshmi and Nobi Ogami. Here, I led an Intensive for a group of twenty or so of Baba's devotees. This was a good icebreaker for me, as I had never led an Intensive before. As things got busier, we spent most of our time at the home of Shambhavi Russell on the slopes of St. Louis Heights, overlooking the city of Honolulu. The view from Shambhavi's home was spectacular at night when the city was all lit up. It was, however, a bit difficult for me as I had no transportation, and I knew Baba wanted me to get out and meet as many people as possible. I assisted Kubera in making phone calls and locating suppliers. Rather than introducing myself on the phone as Swami Sadananda, I began to use the name Samuel Yasi—Sam Yasi for short. Kubera appreciated the humor as I was in fact a sannyasi. This whole process took a few months before the arrival of the main tour staff.

After a long search for a meditation hall for Baba's evening satsangs, we settled on using a large cafeteria at the Kaimuki Elementary School. This was quite the project as the school was in session during the day. As soon as school was out, we began the transformation of the cafeteria to become the meditation hall. All the tables had to be folded up and stored. We acquired large rolls of carpet to cover the entire floor. We hung large photos of Baba and Bhagavan Nityananda on the walls. We purchased just the right size chair and background setup for Baba. We placed large plants and beautiful flowers around the chair. All in all, it looked perfect. After the evening satsang concluded, the entire process had to be reversed. The carpets, the chair, the plants, and all the accessories were stored for the night in the garage of a homeowner who lived directly across the street from the school. The next day the whole process was repeated. A large crew was assigned to this task.

We found a simple home on Kahala Beach for Baba, and another house a little way down the beach for some of his immediate staff. The rest of the traveling party, perhaps twenty or thirty people, rented an old house that had just been vacated at the base of Makiki Heights. This structure was quite dilapidated but livable. It sat on an acre of land, so it gave us a semblance of privacy. It also had fifteen rooms and eleven bathrooms. There were the remnants of a lava stone pool out back that was naturally fed by the rain as it trickled down the cliff. There was also a lovely forty-foot-high avocado tree as well as mango trees adorning the property.

This was a building with some interesting history. It had been built in 1910 by a distant relative of Queen Lili'uokalani, the last sovereign monarch of the Hawaiian Kingdom. The house was known at the time as Rock Cliff Manor. In its heyday, many large gatherings had been hosted on its beautiful Ohi'a wood floors. It also had a wide veranda, ideal for sitting outside.

The carriage house next door was used as a way station and watering place for horses and buggies that were about to travel up nearby Tantalus mountain for the beautiful scenic views at the summit. It was said that the house's original inhabitants had two young children, and that at least one of these children was killed by a carriage coming through. After this terrible accident, the heartbroken family abandoned their home, and the building fell into disrepair.

In the 1940s, the property was purchased by an Irish immigrant, who turned it into a boarding house for gentlemen. Some of the larger rooms were subdivided to make more individual spaces. In time, the owner died, and the property was left to heirs. Then for many years, the building sat unused, and it fell into serious disrepair. For a few decades, it became known as the local "haunted house." Later, neighbors related stories to me of local college fraternities that required new recruits to spend a scary night alone in the house.

By the time we came along, the house was being run by a local priest as a home for women with mental challenges. This group was just moving out when we had a need of the property, and the SYDA Foundation was able to rent it. After an extensive cleanup, Baba's tour staff moved in. This was still a few months before Baba's arrival. The house was in such disrepair that one woman put her foot through a rotted bathroom floor. A staff member came to me one day and said, "Something just isn't right with this room. It feels really creepy in here." I suggested she play a tape of *Shri Guru Gita* in the room throughout the day. She told me the next day that the recording had really helped. Someone described another room, saying, "It feels like the opposite of shakti in there. It has really weird energy." The entire crew chanted the *Shri Guru Gita* in the lobby every morning before work to uplift us and to help change the building's atmosphere.

*　　*　　*

A week or so after Baba arrived, he wanted to see where the staff was staying. He came to the place we were now calling the Makiki House and stopped in the entranceway in front of a large painting of Lakshmi, the goddess of abundance, that had been painted by a local devotee, Roberto Castelli. Baba sweetly said, "Lakshmibai," while making an "okay" sign with his fingers.

Baba's evening satsangs at the Kaimuki Elementary School went very well. Large crowds filled the hall every night. I took my familiar place at the back to help greet and seat people and to answer questions. Baba gave a beautiful Intensive that was well attended by several hundred people. Reporters came from the local newspapers and TV stations to Baba's house to interview him. He was a big hit. I was able to visit Baba frequently at his house on the beach. I loved seeing him just relaxing, watching the wide and peaceful ocean view. He walked on the beach every morning. It was his habit to walk every day, wherever he was.

At some point, Baba called me to his house and told me that I should remain in Honolulu to establish an ashram there, as there were many people who needed a place to pursue their Siddha Yoga practices. We began our search for a suitable location. It wasn't easy to find. At the time, it was felt that the Makiki House was in too much disrepair to even consider.

Kubera and Bill, another sevite, were in charge of searching for a good location. They were coming up empty handed as suitable properties were rare and very expensive. One day at Baba's house, a group of us—including Alvin Shim, a well-known local lawyer—was sitting with Baba. Al was devoted to Baba and was also quite a loving rascal. He spoke up and said, "Baba, why don't you just tell us where the ashram should be. I know you already know!" We laughed. Baba then silently motioned, as if drawing a map in the air, first a straight line, then a curve, then a motion over to the left. Everyone smiled again.

It wasn't more than five minutes later that Bill arrived and said, "I think we've found a place." Al Shim jumped in right away. He started drawing a map in the air as Baba had, and he said, "Is it straight ahead, around a curve, and then over to the left?" Bill was stunned. He said, "Yes! how did you know?" We all had a hearty laugh.

This was at 3807 Diamond Head Circle, a house on the mountain side of Diamond Head Crater. It was ideal for us. It had three large bedrooms suitable for converting to dorms, each with a separate bathroom. It also had a smaller room for me, a large separate kitchen, and a large open room where we could host satsangs for about seventy-five people. There was also a large courtyard shaded by two beautiful banyan trees. In the back of the courtyard, there was a small two-room cottage suitable for a family. We began the process of moving in.

The ashram was right next door to the Unity Church of Hawaii. I had some very nice conversations with the minister of that church over the back fence. He was invited to the inauguration and seemed very moved to meet Baba.

Baba cracked the ceremonial coconut at the front door, and we all went inside with great enthusiasm. I was sitting up front next to Baba when he leaned over and said something to me in Hindi. Malti began to translate for me, but Baba stopped her saying, "Don't translate. He speaks Hindi." He had heard me speaking very elementary Hindi in the courtyard in India. But I didn't understand what he was saying at all, and I leaned in as he repeated his words, "*Kursee lao.*" He was asking me to bring something, but I didn't know what it was. Seeing my frustration, Malti finally translated, "Bring a chair for the reverend." I was a bit shocked to realize I didn't know the Hindi word for chair. In all my years in the courtyard in Ganeshpuri, I had never sat in one. I was quite embarrassed.

Baba then asked me if the new ashram was in a good location. I responded that we were very nicely located in an easily accessible area very close to the Honolulu Zoo.

"The zoo?" Baba replied sternly. "Are we going to be teaching animals now?"

Obviously, I was getting publicly busted. I knew enough to just stay quiet. Everything was okay.

At Baba's house a few days later, Baba was very sweet and gave me the wand of peacock feathers he had been using for darshan. He instructed me to give his touch at the Intensives we were to hold after he left. He also gave me a large Mexican sombrero that someone had given him. He loved hats, and there always seemed to be an endless supply of new and whimsical ones.

It was reported to me by a member of the tour staff that one morning at Baba's house, one of the local trustees had complained to Baba that I was too strict at times. I did always carry with me the discipline with which I had lived in India. Baba's response was, "Don't worry. I made him that way. He can also be very loving. He lived in my courtyard for two years, so he passes all tests."

*   *   *

Finally, the time came for Baba and the tour to leave Hawaii. At the airport, we had a small private room where we were able to wait for boarding. I garlanded Baba with a beautiful lei, which he then gave to Malti. I found it very difficult to think that I wouldn't be seeing him for an unknown period of time and was feeling a bit distraught. I followed him out onto the tarmac toward the plane. I couldn't believe I was staying behind. I was walking so closely behind him that when he turned around and saw me, I had to turn with him. He smiled and said, "The ashram should run with a lot of joy and a lot of love." I took that as my final instruction from him and carried that with me as we built an ashram community.

There was a lot of enthusiasm and excitement in having an ashram in Hawaii, and about a dozen devotees moved in right away. Here, we could pursue spiritual practice with lots of chanting, meditation, and teachings. We quickly became a close family. Kusha, Dan Friedman, became the first ashram manager.

We ate all our meals outside in the beautiful courtyard that was shaded by two large banyan trees. The ashramites spent a lot of time there together. There were a few very young children who either lived in the ashram or came almost every day. Little Shanti and Gopi became an integral part of our community and were deeply loved by us all.

This Siddha Yoga Ashram in Hawaii was thriving. Regular crowds attended satsangs with us. We chanted *Shri Guru Gita* together every morning. Some residents went off to work and those who could remain went about the various tasks of the ashram. Cleaning, cooking, office work, and gardening filled our days. We chanted for half an hour before lunch and in the afternoons some of us would head for a nearby beach or a nice walk. Every evening, we would have a different focus in our satsang. On Monday nights we had readings from a selected scripture. We spent many weeks studying the *Pratyabhijna-hridayam*, a wonderful foundational scripture of Kashmir Shaivism, and then months reading the entire *Jnaneshwari*, which was a favorite of all. Other nights we held great chanting sessions followed by meditation. Saturday night was always a full house as we chanted enthusiastically.

A Siddha Yogi who owned a local radio station gave me a half-hour time slot every week where I interviewed a Siddha Yoga student about their experiences and understanding. This continued for a year or more.

We also started teaching meditation at what was then known as the Oahu Correctional Facility, one of the local prisons. This began with a suggestion from the lawyer Alvin Shim during Baba's stay in Hawaii due to his feeling that there were prisoners who would benefit from meditation instruction. I organized a group to go into the prison and taught several meditation classes there. Later, other Siddha Yogis took over this seva, and we continued to teach meditation classes there for quite a few years.

On his second world tour, in 1975, Baba had given a satsang for two hundred inmates at a prison in Florida. It was shortly after he left Hawaii on his third world tour, while at the Siddha Yoga Ashram in Oakland, California, in 1979, that Baba formally launched the Prison Project. It was adopted by Siddha Yogis across the country. Baba made it possible for prisoners who asked for it to receive the Siddha Yoga Correspondence Course for free. The international Prison Project still exists in numerous locations. Accounts of the experiences and insights written by inmates who participate in the Prison Project have been very inspiring over the years.

Soon, Peggy Bendet, also known as Mahananda, arrived to be our office manager. Years before she had been a reporter for the *Honolulu Star Bulletin*, the major Honolulu newspaper. She brought new skills as she had done a lot of editing for Siddha Yoga books and magazines. She was a big help in writing flyers and brochures. We were also good friends, as she was one of the few who had been to Ganeshpuri and had a deep experience of Siddha Yoga and Baba.

I began to develop one-day workshops and two-day Intensives that alternated once a month on various aspects of the Siddha Yoga teachings. I used to spend three weeks reading and writing in preparation for the next teaching and learning event. After one week to decompress, I would then begin preparation for the next. During the Intensive meditation sessions, according to Baba's instructions to me, I would go around the room and gently swat the participants with the peacock feathers that Baba had given me. I always felt Baba's energy as I did this. Many people also felt his presence in the room. At some point later on, the swamis in the other Siddha Yoga ashrams were all told to stop giving the touch. At that time, I was instructed by Baba to continue doing so. I continued to give Baba's touch during Intensives for quite a few years.

At one point, we decided to do a workshop on Kashmir Shaivism, one of the major philosophical foundations for the Siddha Yoga path. It was an important topic for me to convey successfully as many of the participants were hearing some of this for the first time and others had looked at it only peripherally. Some had taken Siddha Yoga courses with Swami Tejomayananda, who was the foremost speaker on the topic at the time. I was worried that I couldn't convey the depth and meaning of such subtle concepts. I worked hard at my preparation, but I wasn't sure I was going to be able to communicate what I wanted to. The night before the workshop, I had a vivid dream. In the dream, Baba appeared to me and put his entire fist deep into my mouth, all the way down my throat. Then, he pulled out a large wad of cotton. I felt that something deep within me had been physically released. The workshop itself went extremely well. My words and concepts flowed freely. People's comments afterward were very favorable.

After this experience my way of preparing to teach changed significantly. I would still make outlines and write notes for my talks, but I never worried about them again. Also, I became comfortable speaking without notes. I never again needed the same level of preparation.

*　　*　　*

Throughout this time, it was evident that the ashram would need more space and that our house in Diamond Head was a temporary rental location. We were always on the lookout for a more permanent spot. Some days I would drive around various neighborhoods in Honolulu, looking for a potential place. We had numerous realtors searching for us as well. At one point, a realtor suggested that I look at a site in Ka'a'awa, a community about forty minutes from Honolulu on the eastern shore of Oahu. This was a seven-acre plot that stretched from the mountains to the ocean. There were already two beautiful homes on the site, one of which had plenty of open space for a large hall. Buying this property would have been quite expensive, but we began to think of the possibilities. I had the idea that perhaps we could build ten condo units on one side of the property that devotees could purchase, and which could provide us the cost of the property. I spoke to a devotee who was a contractor and to a few people who might be interested, and there was some initial interest in pursuing the idea further. A few weeks later, a devotee received a letter from Baba responding to her letter of great concern that we were going to be so far from our existing site in Honolulu. She was told to tell me that Baba said, "The swami should immediately move to Maui." I didn't take this message literally, but rather to mean, like Maui, this location was too remote. It was the end of any Ka'a'awa plan. We kept searching.

*   *   *

At some point in April of 1980, Baba asked all the swamis to come to Shree Muktananda Ashram in South Fallsburg, New York, for his birthday celebration in May. I had planned to come as well, but I was told that Baba said for me to stay in Honolulu. He said that my work was there. I actually asked three times with the same reply.

Apparently, during the actual celebration, Baba asked one of the swamis, "Where is Swami Sadananda?" This swami reminded Baba that I had asked three times to come and was told not to. I then got a phone call from Baba's attendant, Noni, saying that I was to personally go to the Honolulu airport and meet someone who was bringing something for me. I didn't even know who I was supposed to meet. I went and met the scheduled flight and was very happy to see a woman who was carrying one of Baba's jackets. She was in bliss, having held it in her lap for the entire flight. It was a beautiful orange raw silk jacket with gold-colored buttons. I had seen Baba wearing that jacket in some photos. I was told to wear it, which I did, especially during Intensives. I still have this jacket in my meditation room, and it gives me great joy to remember Baba's amazing gift.

A few weeks later, Lee, one of the ashram residents who worked as a stewardess for Pan American Airways, presented me with a stack of fifteen scratch-off coupons for my birthday. When she was in Honolulu, Lee had been living in the ashram with her sister. Coupons were given to every passenger on her various flights and one lucky person would win a free round-trip ticket to anywhere in the US. As an employee of the airline, Lee was not eligible to win, so she saved the ones she got while traveling as a passenger between scheduled shifts. I was quite surprised as I scratched off each of the tickets to discover that I actually held a winner. I called Baba in South Fallsburg to tell him I had just won a free ticket to New York and that I really wanted to come. Baba happened to be in the office when I called. He said, "Free?" "Yes," I said. He responded. "Free, okay." and I did get the go-ahead. I was thrilled as I hadn't seen Baba in more than two years. I quickly made my plans to be there for one month.

Shree Muktananda Ashram was great. It was wonderful to see Baba again as well as all my dear friends and Siddha Yoga family. Baba was speaking regularly in the new, large, and beautiful hall called Muktananda Mandir. There was a large lake there, dubbed Lake Nityananda, with a delightful walking path. Nature was always giving her bountiful blessings as I strolled around it. It was a wonderful month.

One weekend, a Children's Intensive was being held in the ashram. I got the message at the last minute that I was to walk around the room during the meditation sessions and give "the touch" with Baba's peacock feathers. I did so and felt his blessings as children shared that they had many classic yogic experiences. What a great future was being prepared for a new generation of Siddha Yogis.

As my month-long visit was coming close to an end, I began to feel that I hadn't had any personal time with Baba. I requested a private darshan. This would normally be reserved for special guests or for someone with a unique question for Baba. I was brought into a small waiting room just outside Baba's quarters. Baba came out and sweetly asked, "What is it?" That was when I realized I didn't have a question at all. I said, "I just wanted to see you, Baba." He smiled and responded, "Everything is good. The ashram is good. The trustees are happy. Everything is going well." He then gave me some chocolate as *prasad*, and I left.

*   *   *

When I returned to Honolulu, we continued the search for a new property to put down more permanent roots for the ashram. We also learned that the owners of our present Diamond Head property were preparing to sell it. The new buyers wanted to tear the building down and put up a large family complex. That added some pressure to find something soon. Toward the end of the summer, one of the Hawaii trustees was visiting Baba in South Fallsburg. At the end of his stay, Baba told him to tell me to "go get that old building in Makiki." I was thrilled with this as I had mentioned it so many times over the past few years at our trustee meetings that I thought people were getting tired of hearing me bring it up. Now, it was a reality. The problem, of course, was to consider what it would cost and what it would take to renovate it.

I asked three local carpenters who were Siddha Yogis to evaluate the building for renovation, and I also began discussions with the owners, who I suspected would be interested in working with us. The carpenters gave me their best estimate for repairs. Knowing that there are always unknowns with a property like this, I tripled their numbers and took that as what we would need. The ashram had saved some money from the various Intensives and workshops I had given. There were also donations and revenue from the residents who lived in our current location.

We came up with a plan that we could rent the facility on a long-term lease with a first option to buy it later at fair market value, minus the cost of the renovations we were planning to do. After some negotiations, we were finally able to close the deal, and we drew up the necessary papers. As the director of SYD Hawaii, I signed a twelve-year lease, and the work began. We definitely had a very big project ahead of us.

We recruited a crew of carpenters and plumbers from the ashram in Oakland as well as local workers from Maui and Oahu. The local devotees pitched in regularly, and there was often a large crew working very hard and with great devotion. The community came together for this project. Walls had to be removed to create a large hall for satsangs. Everything had to be updated. We expanded a downstairs bathroom to be two separate bathrooms, suitable for men and women. The flooring was repaired. Painting was done throughout. The existing roof had to be torn off and replaced—and that job expanded when we found that there were several roofs on the building, one set on top of the other. In the walls, we had to deal with leftover Paris Green in the rafters, which is a powdery arsenic compound used to repel termites. We sanded and polished the old Hawaiian Ohi'a wood floors in the entrance area to look beautiful and new. The main hall was carpeted with a beautiful, lush navy carpet. Ed Torgerson made a gorgeous backdrop for Baba's chair and a matching one for the rear altar out of koa wood. Beautiful photos of Baba chanting and of some of the other siddhas that are respected in our tradition were hung. The walls were soundproofed to minimize disturbance to our neighbors. Debris had to be taken to the dump at least once daily.

Then there was the landscaping. We had the final plan drawn up by a well-known local landscape artist. There was an old coconut tree stump that stood in the way of our plan on the far end of the property. We rented a small backhoe and relied on the friend of a devotee who agreed to do the job of stump removal. The backhoe was delivered but the night before the project was to begin, we received a call that the operator of the backhoe couldn't make it.

I decided that I would try to figure it out and got up early to learn how to operate the machine myself. There wasn't a manual, and operating large equipment hadn't been taught in my sannyasa training. I figured out the basic controls while having people stand way back. Working slowly, I was able to dig out that stubborn stump. Everything was going great until I lifted a four-inch diameter sewer pipe, ten feet in the air. Fortunately, we had Arun, the plumber, on hand for a quick repair. The new plantings were beautiful. A variety of travelers palms, tall ferns, and many varieties of tropical plants and flowers now adorned our new home.

I designed a waterfall for the main entrance where Baba acknowledged the large painting of Goddess Lakshmi during his visit to the house. Sabra, a ceramic artist, made beautiful tiles with symbols of all the major religions on them. These were inlaid on the three steps leading up to the waterfall. The waterfall itself was made from large local lava stones gathered and placed by Hunton Conrad from Maui. We placed a sandalwood statue of Lakshmi there to commemorate Baba's visit and his honoring of Lakshmi at that exact spot.

The entire project was massive—bigger than anyone had imagined—yet we did it all in just a few months. Photos were taken throughout the project. At a heart-opening finale, the photos were presented in a slide show with two alternating projectors, accompanied by the song "Ride Like the Wind," by Christopher Cross. A perfect choice. The exhausted crew cheered!

At the inauguration, which I recall was in February of 1981, a Siddha Yoga swami came from Los Angeles to join us, and the whole community rejoiced in our accomplishment. Regular satsangs grew in attendance, as we now had more room to expand in our stunningly beautiful hall. About three hundred people in our community came at various times. Intensive and workshop participant numbers also grew.

I began speaking more frequently at a few local colleges and at the University of Hawaii. I was invited to the Pearl Harbor Naval Base to speak to a group of servicemen who were in a special program for men who were facing disciplinary action. They had been given a six-week series of self-help programs to help them find a more positive path. I was with them for three hours during one day of the program and taught them meditation. I did this every few weeks for a year or more. These sessions were always rated their favorite.

Our ashram community had become quite close. Our programs and work forged a bond that was palpable, and many friendships are still intact today. We studied together, learned together, and reveled in Baba's grace and the Siddha Yoga teachings. To do this in Hawaii was an added treat. Life was good.

23. PASSING ON THE LINEAGE

In mid-1981, Baba announced in a public program that young Swami Nityananda would be his successor. We were all quite surprised as he was a very easygoing sort of fellow in contrast to Baba's dynamic personality. Nityananda was Malti's younger brother by eight years. He had been given sannyasa a few months before with a group of Westerners. Baba said that Malti would also be given sannyasa at a later date in a special ceremony. By February of 1982 he announced that Malti would join young Nityananda as co-successor. I don't think anyone could really fathom that Baba would ever actually be gone.

A formal ceremony, called the *pattabhishek*, was scheduled for Baba's birthday celebration in May of 1982 to install both successors. A few weeks before the installation ceremony, Malti was given *brahmacharya diksha*, the initiation that traditionally is given before sannyasa. Baba himself participated in her *brahmacharya* ceremony. Her head was shaved at that time, and she was given the traditional white robes to wear.

I arrived in India from Honolulu only a day or two before the pattabhishek. I had not been in Ganeshpuri since June of 1978 when I was first sent to Hawaii. I was very happy to be there. I was just arriving at my room on the top floor of the Guru Chowk building when Malti appeared, walking with a group of swamis who had also just arrived from around the world. I was greeted joyfully by my swami family. Malti was in white robes with her head shaven. She took my hand in the way friends would often hold hands in India—with interlocked pinkies—and held it as we walked across the hallway. Quite surprised but quite pleased, I knew I was home.

A few days later, Malti was initiated into sannyasa and was given a renunciant's orange robes and the name Swami Chidvilasananda, meaning "the bliss of the play of consciousness."

Following this was the pattabhishek itself: an elaborate ceremony, presided over by a group of Brahmins at the culmination of a *yajna*, a traditional fire ceremony. There were large crowds present to witness this historic event. When Baba walked into the hall, there was a sudden clap of thunder, and an intense rainstorm broke out. In India this would be considered an auspicious sign at a yajna. It is not at all common for there to be rain in May. It was the hot season, and everything was normally completely dry. We all shouted out with glee, along with Baba, "*Sadgurunath Maharaj ki Jai!*" the jubilant phrase of invocation in Siddha Yoga satsangs and ceremonies. Baba said, "The rains have come to welcome them." Baba looked so proud of his two successors.

The swamis had all planned to be in the ashram for one month. Toward the end of that time, we were all gathered in the courtyard sitting with Baba. At one point Baba called me up to him. He spoke so sweetly to me and said that I should stay for a while longer and that he would let me know when it was time to return to Hawaii. While he was speaking to me, he was holding my left hand and was playing with my wrist mala that I wore. As his feet were outstretched, I then massaged his feet while he spoke. It seemed most natural for me to do this. I was told to talk to one of the other swamis to decide who to send to Honolulu in my place. After some consideration it was decided to send Swami Turiyananda, who was the youngest of the swamis and quite bright.

My one-month stay turned into five. In some ways, this was a hard time for me. I didn't have a specific role to play, and I never quite found the right avenue of seva. I gave a talk one weekend afternoon in the Guru Chowk hall to a large group of Indians and Westerners. It was called "Balance in Sadhana" and was very well received. Baba seemed very pleased and commented afterward that I spoke very well.

During these months, my relationship with Baba deepened. I'd always idolized him as an image of perfection and everything I ever wanted to be, and I was very attached to his physical form. Having spent time away from him in Hawaii, my practices had matured, and I now began to focus on my inner experience of his teachings. Baba always taught that the guru is not the physical form but is the shakti. The energy that flows through the guru's form is the true guru. I was now experiencing that on a profound level.

Baba began to treat me as a friend, and he would sometimes call for me at any odd time and just talk. He would sometimes talk about the weather or introduce me to guests who were there and tell them what a beautiful ashram I had built in Hawaii. Baba frequently said how pleased he was that I had built the ashram without ever asking for any money. When he first left me in Hawaii, he had given me five thousand dollars and said I should ask for more if I needed it. I never asked for another penny.

This went on through mid-September 1982 when Baba held an Intensive at the Taj Mahal Hotel in Bombay, just prior to his leaving for a trip to Kashmir. I was at the Intensive with a group of swamis. As we had done every night in the ashram, the swamis would gather in Baba's room to chant a special set of mantras with him. One evening following this chant, I took the opportunity to ask Baba a question that had been urgently posed by a devotee back in Hawaii. Baba responded and then said it was now time for me to return to Honolulu. "You built a beautiful ashram," he said. "Your work is there."

Dada Yande was in the room, and Baba told him to give me prasad. Dada began to give me some *sev*, which is like a party mix of dried grains and spices. I held out my chanting card to be able to hold the pile Dada was offering. Baba kept saying, "Give him more. Give him more," repeatedly until the pile grew to such a massive amount on my chanting card that I could hardly hold it. Baba then looked at me with great love and tenderness and said, "You should eat all of it and don't have dinner tonight." He then said, "Don't waste time. Make arrangements to go right away."

An arrangement was made for me to spend the night in Bombay with a devotee so I could immediately apply for my exit visa and get airplane tickets. Everything fell into place easily. Within a week, I was all set to go. I was eager to return to Hawaii. At the time I didn't know that this would be my final darshan with Baba.

24. Mahasamadhi, 1982

I arrived back in Honolulu and began to settle in. Swami
Turiyananda had done a good job of maintaining the ashram and
the community seemed to like him. All was going along nicely for
about two weeks until one morning during the *Shri Guru Gita*
recitation, I was called out for an urgent telephone call. One of
Baba's ashram managers was on the phone to tell me that Baba had
taken *mahasamadhi*, the term used when a yogi of his stature had
died. I was told to return to Ganeshpuri right away. After the
recitation, I gathered everyone together to tell them the news. We
were all in a bit of a shock. Swami Turiyananda and I managed to get
a flight that evening via Singapore. I knew the ashram was in good
hands as Bhadra and Ajit were there as assistant managers.

We arrived in Bombay around two o'clock in the morning and
reached the ashram in Ganeshpuri by around four. We were
immediately ushered into Baba's room, where his body was being
prepared for internment. Baba was in a sitting position on a raised
bed. It looked as if he was peacefully meditating. Turiyananda and I
sat for two hours with Baba's form in his bedroom until a flight from
New York arrived with a large group of devotees, who then filled the
room. At that time Bhau Shastri, who had performed so many
special yajnas and pujas over the years, began the final *abhishek*, a
ritual bath with the recitation of many special mantras. A few people
were quietly sobbing. There was a general sense of peace that filled
the room. Afterward Baba's body was placed on a throne and carried
out of the ashram to a waiting flatbed vehicle to be taken to the
village of Ganeshpuri for a final darshan at the shrine where his
beloved guru, Bhagavan Nityananda, was entombed. Thousands of

people in the street accompanied the vehicle, which slowed to a crawl as we walked behind. Many had come from Bombay for this event. People were showering Baba with hundreds of garlands as we passed, and cries of "*Sadgurunath Maharaj ki Jay*" resounded through the streets. Swamis Chidvilasananda and Nityananda were on the vehicle with Baba's body. It must have been two hours before we were able to slowly make our way back to the ashram.

Six months prior to this, Baba had the walls removed from his original meditation room, which Bhagavan Nityananda had had built for him some forty years before. Without the walls, there was now a large open room that was to be Baba's final resting place. He had known that his time was near and in fact he had told this to a number of ashram trustees. Baba wanted to remain forever in the place where his guru had originally told him to stay.

His body, in a seated position, was carefully lowered into the opening that had been dug at the spot of his original seat. Bhau Shastri continued the appropriate rituals and mantras as hundreds offered their blessings. Some people tossed their *malas* or other sacred objects into the open pit with their guru. I placed my treasured wrist mala there.

Great quantities of salt were then poured into the pit to begin covering Baba's body. As I saw him slowly disappear beneath a mountain of salt, I began to realize that my beloved Baba was actually gone. I would not see him again—at least not physically. The final layers of earth were placed on top of the tomb, and he was gone. Many people recounted stories of great insight and spiritual communion during the coming days. For me, I felt only the profound sadness of losing Baba. I loved him dearly. I understood that what he had given me could never leave, but I still knew I would miss his physical presence.

A chant of *Om Namo Bhagavate Muktanandaya* was sustained all day and all night for thirty days. Around this chant, the days were filled with all the regular tasks of everyday ashram life.

Every evening after dark both Swami Chidvilasananda and Swami Nityananda would sit on a double chair in the courtyard next to Baba's seat. Lights were off as people began coming up for their darshan of the two gurus. There was a line for each. People chose the line that was the most comfortable for them. I watched this from a distance for a few nights and by the fifth night I felt I should show my respects to Baba's successors. I chose to go on the line for Swami Chidvilasananda as I felt more aligned with her more traditional style. I finally reached her position and bowed deeply with my head to the ground to honor her. Unexpectedly, she then placed both of her feet on my head. I felt that it was a true blessing and an acceptance by her. Gradually this became more real for me as I recognized that this was the future of the Siddha Yoga path. I wanted very much to remain a part of it. The month-long chant in honor of Baba continued day and night. From my room I could hear the chant even when I wasn't in the hall. It was a time to assimilate the recent events with both sadness and introspection.

After a few more weeks I began to feel that I should return to Honolulu. I thought the ashram community there needed me to give perspective and support. I spoke to Gurumayi, and she agreed. I made my plans.

25. Gurumayi Comes to Hawaii, 1983

I was happy to be home. I loved Hawaii. My role was clear, and the day-to-day administration of the ashram and my teaching schedule were a great comfort to me. I felt truly grateful that I'd had that final darshan with Baba before he left. The community was adjusting to the changes, and all in all, things were good. However, there was a lot to adapt to. I began to feel a new freedom and an unfettering of the longing to always be with Baba. I began to internalize my relationship with the guru even more, while remembering that Baba had always said the guru is not the physical form but the energy of grace that flows through that physical form. This was a time for deep reflection.

In early 1983, both Swami Chidvilasananda, now affectionately called Gurumayi, and young Swami Nityananda arrived in Hawaii during their first world tours. They had arrived, both from India but via different directions. One had gone west through Europe and the other east through Australia. They united in Honolulu. Prior to their arrivals, we had big preparations to make. A suitable house was rented in Lanikai, which was my personal favorite part of the island. It is a gorgeous stretch of beach with a calm, relaxed atmosphere. In the Hawaiian language, *Lanikai* means "heaven by the sea." A group of sevites cleaned and prepared rooms for the two gurus, and we booked a large hall in a Waikiki hotel for their evening satsangs. When Gurumayi arrived, the first thing she asked me was if I had gotten any sleep that night. In fact, quite a few of us had been up all night making last-minute preparations. I said no, and she smiled a sweet smile of compassion.

I was called to their house in Lanikai one morning and sat with the two of them as they expressed a dilemma. It seemed that Gurumayi liked to start her satsangs with a fifteen-minute chant of the mantra *Om Namah Shivaya*, while Nityananda liked to start his satsangs by singing the five-minute prayer *Jyota se Jyota Jagao* (Kindle My Heart's Flame with Your Flame.) They asked for my opinion about how they should open their joint satsangs in Honolulu. After a moment's thought, I suggested that we chant *Om Namah Shivaya* for ten minutes and then sing *Jyota se Jyota Jagao*. They looked at each other and smiled, and that was what we decided to do. The evening satsangs were very well attended. Hundreds of people came every night.

A few months later, I received word that some of the smaller ashrams around the country were to be closed. I was told that the intention was to refocus energy on the larger ashrams and to encourage Siddha Yoga students to concentrate on their own practice. I got a call from Swami Nityananda saying that I was to be transferred to the Siddha Yoga Ashram in Oakland and that someone else—another swami—would be assigned to Hawaii. This came as a great shock to me. I told Swami Nityananda about my final darshan with Baba and how he had said that my work was in Hawaii. I explained that I held onto Baba's words as a final instruction from him.

Nityananda responded that he and Gurumayi had been told by Baba that they could make whatever changes they considered necessary.

Initially, this instruction from the new head of my spiritual path upended my sense of purpose. I had clung to the idea that I would be in Hawaii forever. A few devotees wrote letters to plead the case for me to stay in Hawaii. I took a long walk alone to process what was happening. During this walk, I reached the point where I could accept this decision from the two gurus, and I surrendered to the fact that I would be leaving Hawaii. It would be okay.

About an hour after I returned from this walk, I received a phone call from Swami Kripananda, who relayed the message on the

Guru's behalf that, in fact, I should stay in Hawaii. I told her to convey that I was resigned to leave if that's what was wanted.

Swamiji said, "It's okay to stay."

I was relieved, but I also had to face the reality that the time might come when the ashram in Honolulu would close or I would be reassigned. I began to contemplate what I would do under those circumstances.

At some point in the following year, young Nityananda decided he no longer wanted to be a swami and stepped down from his position. A year later, he reversed his decision, put on sannyasa robes again, and formed his own organization, ashram, and path.

In late 1983, I accompanied a group of nineteen Siddha Yogis from Hawaii to visit Gurumayi in the ashram in Ganeshpuri. This was a memorable visit for everyone. Most had never been to India before, and this *yatra*—this pilgrimage—gave everyone a deeper experience of the Siddha Yoga path and of their own spiritual practices.

Time went on. The immediacy of any change for me faded, but the possibility was always in the back of my mind. In some ways, I was feeling free of all roles. I wondered what the future held for me. These feelings became stronger, and then came a point when I felt I was at a crossroads.

I was still committed to Siddha Yoga as a spiritual path and yet, I felt untethered from the form it was to take for me. I wrestled with this for quite some time. Nothing could change the depth of experience I had and yet, I saw increasingly that I could choose to express it in different ways.

My commitment to Baba and the role I was given was profound and unique. I had taken formal vows. Being a swami always felt very natural to me. I was most myself in that role. I also began to see that this was just another mental construct. Baba so often spoke of the need to integrate spirituality into our ordinary lives. I had done so considerably, yet I began to feel confined by the role I was in. I had to reconcile my commitment to Baba and to sannyasa with a growing need to express myself in new ways. I went through a lot of soul searching as to what I really wanted. Each day at the top of my mind was this serious consideration of my reasons to stay versus what my deepest heart was telling me to do.

Laura, then known as Bhadra, who had been the ashram's finance manager, had become a good friend and confidant. We grew closer together as I shared my dilemma with her. We understood each other and had a natural connection. I began to see that there was a possibility of our having a deeper relationship. I could now see that I wouldn't be in Hawaii forever and that I had a choice to make. I wrote to Gurumayi and told her that I wanted to take some time off to consider things. My mother, back in New York, was having surgery and needed some assistance. My plan was to start there and see what developed. I told the local community of my plans, and that my future was uncertain. Bhadra had already decided to leave Hawaii to be with her family on the East Coast. We made plans to contact each other at some point.

Early in the morning of the day that I was to leave Honolulu, a *Shri Guru Gita* recitation was held on the beach with a large group of devotees. There were a lot of tears and good wishes expressed. It was a beautiful and heartfelt send off.

PART FIVE—LIVING IN GRATITUDE

26. A NEW LIFE, 1984

My first stop was in Los Angeles, where I spent a few days in the Siddha Yoga ashram, where Gurumayi was at the time. I had hoped to have an opportunity to speak with Gurumayi. I requested a meeting and was told to wait in a hallway outside of a room she was in. I sat there for quite some time and finally was told that I couldn't see her just then. I took it as an indication that I should trust myself and make up my own mind. Soon after, I left for New York.

Laura was also passing through New York on her way to her parents' home in Pittsburgh. She stayed at my mother's house and helped tend to my mother's needs. I decided to travel with her to Pittsburgh. Our relationship was becoming real. It seemed my choice had been made. Laura and I went to Little Compton, Rhode Island, where her close friend and former college roommate, Liz Peckham, lived with her husband, Skip Paul. Liz's family owned a 150-year-old farm and greenhouse. They lived near the greenhouse and had a small organic farm themselves. Laura and I stayed with them for a few weeks.

At some point, in late August or early September, I heard that Gurumayi, who had been in the Siddha Yoga Ashram in South Fallsburg, was going to be leaving for India in a few days. I immediately jumped in my car and headed for New York. I really wanted to speak to her before she left. I arrived and requested a meeting and was asked to wait in Swami Kripananda's room. I was quite nervous about speaking with Gurumayi, but I wanted to be open and up-front about everything.

When Gurumayi came in, I told her that I wanted to be honorably released from sannyasa. She asked where I was living. I told her that I was in Rhode Island and that Laura was also there. It was a very emotional conversation. I was in tears talking to her. I told her that this really felt like the right thing for me. I said, "How could it not be if it feels so right?" She said, "*Maya* is very strong." Maya, of course, is the power of illusion. Gurumayi was also very sympathetic and kind. We spoke a bit more for a while and then she gave me some chocolate as prasad. I drove back to Rhode Island with a full heart.

Gurumayi left for India the next day. The following evening, I received a phone call from Bombay. Gurumayi had one of her secretaries call me as soon as they touched down. The message was that if I wanted to come to Ganeshpuri for a month to consider my plans, a ticket would be provided. I thought very carefully about this invitation but then sent Gurumayi a letter telling her that I felt that I needed to follow my original plans.

*   *   *

Once again, I was beginning a new chapter of my life. I had no idea how I was going to live or support myself. I began to create a résumé that described my background and skills. At the time I had only two years of undergraduate study, having left college some fifteen years earlier. I felt, however, that I had life skills and experience that could help me fit in somewhere. I just had no idea where.

Laura's friend Liz knew of a career counseling company in Providence, Rhode Island, called Options, Inc. The owner had lived in Little Compton. This seemed like a good place to start, and I made an appointment to talk to a counselor. When I arrived, I was told that my assigned counselor had a scheduling conflict, and that the owner of the company, Natalie Joslin, would be seeing me instead. Natalie and I seemed to hit it off right away. She had a daughter who had spent time with a yoga group, and Natalie had visited this daughter and had even learned some meditation and yoga herself. So, she understood my background. After a few minutes of conversation, she began asking me a lot of questions. I began to detect a different tone in her voice. I said to her, "It sounds to me that you are suggesting that you might have an opportunity for me here. Am I reading that right?" She responded, "Well, you are very intuitive. I have been searching for a new counselor for some time. I have met many people who have all the right professional credentials but just not the right personal qualities. You have none of the formal credentials, but you have all the other qualities I have been looking for."

She then gave me a task. She offered to pay me $100 a day for three days to do a small study she was interested in. As a career counseling company, she was interested in exploring the possibility of expanding her services to assist the disabled population in their career searches. She wanted me to test the waters a bit to determine if this was feasible. I readily accepted the task.

Not knowing much about the local situation in Providence, I began to call around to the relevant people and groups. In just a few days I spoke to the Department of Labor and visited four or five local organizations and professionals who dealt with that population. They were all interested in the proposition but said there were no available funds to help make such a project happen. With Laura's help, I organized and wrote up my findings. I was then asked by Natalie to present my study to her staff. She wanted them to meet me.

When I arrived, I was ushered into a conference room. I was a comfortable public speaker by this point, but in this case, I was being asked to speak to a staff of seven business professionals. They were graduates of Harvard, Yale, and the Wharton School of Business, and they all had specialty degrees in career development. My presentation went well, and I seemed to have Natalie's approval as she advocated for me.

There was still some tension in the room though, especially from Harry who was a graduate of Yale. At one point he actually pounded the table with his fist as he said, "We are hearing all these nice things about your background. Tell me one bad thing about yourself!"

There was a heightened unease in the room as everyone turned to me. What would I say to that? After a few seconds of thought, I responded casually, "It's very likely that no one in this room will be able to read my handwriting." Everyone breathed a sigh of relief as did I. It seemed that was the right kind of answer to a difficult question. It was true but not disqualifying for the situation.

Natalie spoke up and said she wanted to hire me and train me to be their new career counselor. Harry didn't speak to me for about six months as I was taking over some of his responsibilities. I was trained by Wesley Merritt, who had been a lead counselor at Drake Beam Morin, Inc. of Boston, the largest career development and outplacement services company in the country. There were two sides to our company. Options, Inc., did individual career counseling, mostly with professionals who were making second career choices, as well as younger men and women who were looking for direction to help begin their careers. The other side of the company was a branch office of Right Associates, Inc., which did corporate outplacement work. They assisted large companies in the process of downsizing by offering support to their workers in obtaining new positions or in changing careers. I worked mostly on the Options side and also did special projects with Right Associates.

After a few months of training, I began to see some clients of my own. I was also trained to administer and interpret the personality profiles we used to assist in this process. This led into a sales process for our various programs. I was good at all this and made some significant contributions overall. I also taught meditation to the staff and clients in group sessions, which was well received.

By November, Laura and I decided to marry. With just three weeks' notice we invited our immediate families and a few friends to the small church in the center of the town of Little Compton, Rhode Island. We were married on November 24, 1984. It was a beautiful wedding, and we were very happy.

I worked for Options, Inc. for the next four and a half years. I am still so grateful to Natalie Joslin for giving me that first opportunity. I think of her as Lakshmi, the goddess of wealth and good fortune. Her reaching out to me was really an act of grace. I felt so blessed. The synchronicity of events and opportunities was amazing. I felt that the blessings of both Baba and Gurumayi were behind me. My meditations were deep. I also learned a lot about what it meant to work as a professional.

I did well there, but after about four years, I began to feel that this wasn't the final position for me. I was doing the self-evaluation that we always recommended to our clients. We taught that once a year it is useful to review your job and your future plans in order to ensure you are on the right track. I decided that regardless of whether I was going to stay or not, I needed to pick up the educational credits I was lacking. If there were ever changes in the company, I could be the first to be let go, as I had the fewest academic credentials. After I made a firm decision to return to school, I began to explore what course of study I wanted to pursue.

I found that some colleges would give credit for life experience. I could have gotten a degree in counseling within two years. I wasn't sure, however, that this is what I wanted. After so many years of teaching and counseling, I wanted something that was more tangible. I didn't really feel at home in the business or corporate environment, but I also didn't know where else to apply my skills.

*   *   *

During this time, Gurumayi was staying in the Siddha Yoga Ashram in Boston for ten days. The ashram was just an hour drive north of Providence. While Gurumayi was there, Laura and I drove to the ashram every evening after work. Usually, we got there after the talks and chanting were over but just in time for Gurumayi's darshan. She would often greet us very sweetly saying, "Ah, the couple." It was wonderful to see Gurumayi. One day she told Laura to cook delicious food for me and told me to comb Laura's hair. I felt she was telling us to take care of each other. I really appreciated Gurumayi's acceptance and good wishes for us.

One day in the ashram, I ran into a young man I had known peripherally in India. He had recently graduated from chiropractic college and was doing extremely well in his practice in North Adams, Massachusetts. This piqued my interest, and I decided to explore the possibility of a chiropractic career for myself. It seemed to check all the boxes. It was uplifting work that was beneficial to many people. It was something tangible that I would do with my hands after years of teaching and counseling. It was also quite lucrative, and I could work for myself. I began to seek out and meet with local chiropractors, and I liked what I saw. The more I saw, the more I liked.

Laura and I decided to visit a few chiropractic colleges to see what it would actually take to do this. I found out that a chiropractic degree would require four years of advanced training. There was a chiropractic college in New York State, but I didn't want to live in New York. I was always happy to be *from* New York. We visited the Palmer College of Chiropractic in Davenport, Iowa, which was the first chiropractic college and where the profession began. We then visited Logan College of Chiropractic in St. Louis, Missouri, and really liked it there. I applied for admission and was accepted.

As it turned out I first had to complete some additional science credits as prerequisites before starting the main program. I had some credits from my earlier schooling, but I still needed a full year each of General Chemistry, Organic Chemistry, and Physics before I could begin. Fortunately, there are feeder schools where this can be completed in an accelerated six months as is common in a summer session schedule. That meant a full year of course material condensed into six months. I found that if I took the first half of General Chemistry in night school while still in Rhode Island, I could shave six months off the schedule in St. Louis. I proceeded to register at Rhode Island Community College night school.

When I got there, I was told that, since I had been out of college for over fifteen years, I couldn't take General Chemistry without first taking a remedial mathematics course. However, that would have negated the ability to save time in St. Louis. I requested that I be allowed to take the course anyway and was told I needed special permission from the dean of the Science Department. The dean was quite gruff as she said, "Mr. Auerbach, what I'm trying to tell you is that your chances of getting a D in this course without remedial math are slim to none!" (D would have been a barely passing grade.)

I responded, "Yes, but if I pay the fee, will you let me take it anyway?" She was not happy about this, but she relented.

I then went to speak with the professor who would be teaching the course. I asked him if I was being reasonable. Could I really be okay attempting this?

He told me, "You would have to work very hard, but there is no gauge of what sheer drive and determination can accomplish." I believe those are the wise words of a true educator. I really appreciated that.

I began taking the class in the evenings after work.

It truly was hard. Algebraic equations were mind-boggling to me. I had always been good in the sciences, but I had never liked math. Geometry and trigonometry were somewhat easier for me back in high school, but I never studied any of the higher math courses. I can remember sitting in my room in Rhode Island and literally banging my head on my desk in tears. Why couldn't I do this? How would I get through this? I was determined to succeed, but I felt blocked. Finally, one day I decided to take this issue into my meditation. I tried to trace my dislike of math to its root. A memory arose of me being in first or second grade and being asked to memorize the basic multiplication tables. I just didn't want to. My father sent me into my parents' bedroom, saying, "Don't come out until you have learned the first half." About four hours later, he came in to check on me and found me playing with my pencil. I hadn't learned a thing.

As I recalled this, I realized that, at that very moment, I had decided to not learn and to not like math. I had just shut off that part of my brain. As I contemplated this and offered it to my higher Self, I felt the pattern release. I was gradually able to work with this. Today, I do most math in my head. I still had to work very hard, and it certainly was drive and determination that got me through. I was thrilled to see that at the end of the course I had gotten an A.

With the application of a little common sense, I also immediately enrolled in a remedial math course to catch up.

27. ST. LOUIS, MISSOURI, 1988

When Laura and I set off to St Louis, both sets of our parents thought we were crazy to uproot ourselves like this. We had seemed settled in Rhode Island. We both had good jobs. Laura had been applying her master's in education degree, first in a teaching position and then at a bank. Two years earlier, we had purchased our first home. Nevertheless, a new adventure was calling.

I enrolled in a program at St. Louis Community College that was a feeder program for both Logan Chiropractic College and a nearby nursing school. Here, I could complete the rest of the prerequisites that I needed to begin my training. The work wasn't easy, but I managed to get through all the preliminary courses. Now, the real work of chiropractic study was to begin.

By taking all the summer sessions, it was possible for a person to complete the four-year, ten trimesters of chiropractic study in three and a half years. In fact, most students did it that way. My days were filled with Gross Anatomy (including full human dissection), Spinal Anatomy, Biochemistry, Neuroanatomy, Physiology, Cardiology, Pathology, Microbiology, as well as learning the vital techniques of spinal adjusting. Along with all of this I continued to meditate every morning before classes began. I don't think I could have gotten through it without the grounding effect of meditation.

Meanwhile, Laura took a job in the office of a local chiropractor to learn the ins and outs of the management side of chiropractic. She also became certified as a chiropractic assistant through a course at Logan College.

By 1989, while I was in my second trimester of study, we were expecting a child. We were very much looking forward to this as

Laura had suffered a miscarriage a year before. Now, she was due in the second week of July. A few days before the baby was born, I had a vivid dream of Bhagavan Nityananda. He and I were on a raft in the middle of the ocean. He suddenly stood up and dove into the water. He then surfaced, holding a baby boy just as I woke up.

*   *   *

Baby Jason was born with all the signs of a healthy, beautiful boy. Laura and I were both elated. By the time Jason was born, Laura and I had been up for more than twenty-four hours. After we'd spent a few hours with him, the nurses recommended that they take the child to the nursery to allow us to get a little rest. We agreed as we were both exhausted. As I laid down to rest, I was contemplating the journey I had been on. I was remembering my time with Baba, and my thoughts turned to my sannyasa initiation. Clear memories of that early morning at the river where the morning star shone so bright as we offered our lives to the highest truth and to the service of humanity. I marveled at how Laura and I had brought new life into the world. I offered my thoughts of the situation to Baba. I offered myself, my wife, and my newborn child to God, and I drifted off to sleep.

We were awakened a few hours later by the pediatrician coming into the room. This was not normal. Laura immediately asked, "Is he alive?"

The doctor said, "Yes, but we are concerned about brain damage. He was found in his nursery crib face down and unresponsive." They were waiting for a helicopter to arrive to fly Jason to a neonatal intensive care unit a few miles away at St. Louis Children's Hospital.

I was immediately taken to a room where I saw that Jason was intubated and surrounded by a team of doctors using a manual oxygen pump. I leaned over Jason, near his head, and was talking to him. I remember saying, "Please come back. We have great toys and a good life waiting for you. We love you so very much." I remember one of the doctors choking with emotion as I spoke. For me, it was as if a thief had come in the night. The doctors did their best to revive him, but to no avail. It had been a busy night in the nursery full of newborns. The staff may have paid less attention to Jason as he looked so perfectly healthy and strong. Even though we were planning to breastfeed, the staff had given him a bottle of glucose water in the nursery. Laura had had gestational diabetes during her pregnancy, meaning her blood sugar was temporarily high. When a child is born under those conditions, his blood sugar can go low after he is cut off from his mother's high level of blood glucose. When the staff gave him the glucose water, his blood sugar likely rose sharply and then went very low, putting him into danger of severe hypoglycemia, coma, and death. Later, the lab records confirmed this.

I called the ashram in Ganeshpuri and left a message for Gurumayi. Soon, I received a return message, saying, "Be strong and remember God. Keep me updated." This was a source of strength for us. A bit later, a kind doctor came into our room to ask how we were doing. His exact words were, "Be strong and remember God." Echoing Gurumayi as they did, the doctor's words to us provided some additional comfort. We then went to be with Jason at St. Louis Children's Hospital, where he had been placed on life support.

The doctors did everything possible, but the next morning we were told that his kidneys and other vital organs were failing and that there was no brain activity. We were told to come right away. There was no hope. He was gone.

We called Ganeshpuri with the update. Hemananda Argent, one of Gurumayi's secretaries, answered. She was in the upper gardens at the time. Just as we began speaking, she said, "Wait, Gurumayi is just walking by." Gurumayi got on the phone with us, and I told her what was happening. She spoke very compassionately and then said that, when it was possible, Laura and I should both come to Ganeshpuri.

At the Children's Hospital, we were allowed to spend some time alone with our son. Laura and I together held Jason in our arms for a long while, and when we were ready, the doctor came in to remove his breathing tube. We then watched the last moments of his life slip away. It was a great loss. Even in the midst of this, we felt a profound aura of peace and Gurumayi's blessing. We felt that Gurumayi had transported us to a place beyond pain.

At the time, I was three weeks away from my mid-term exams. We scheduled the trip to India as soon as we could. The school had a two-week break between trimesters over the Christmas holiday, and this was the ideal time for us to go to India. It wasn't easy to continue studying for my exams, but I suppose it was good to be kept busy. I got through it all, and we soon left for India.

When we arrived in Ganeshpuri, Gurumayi greeted us very warmly. She had arranged for Bhau Shastri Vaijapurkar, who had performed so many fire ceremonies in the ashram for many years, to do a special puja for me. I was taken to Tapovan, an area at the very back of the ashram on top of a hill. Here, Bhau Shastri and his young assistant spent four hours alone with me, performing an elaborate ceremony of mantras and prayers to officially release me from the vows of sannyasa that I had taken.

The next day, Laura and I were taken to an area in the upper garden near Turiya Mandir, where Bhau Shastri and his assistant performed a Shanti Puja for the two of us. During this ceremony, all the planets in our respective astrological charts were propitiated to bring about peace in our lives. It was a beautiful gesture on Gurumayi's part. She even gave me special clothes to wear for this ceremony. Right after this puja, Bhau Shastri performed a marriage ceremony for Laura and me. We then returned to the courtyard and offered Gurumayi a beautiful garland of fragrant flowers and our truly grateful hearts. I will never forget Gurumayi's generosity and compassion. It was a very healing time. We left India on New Year's Day 1990.

*   *   *

As part of my tenth and final trimester of school I was required to work in a chiropractic office for two months as an externship. I got permission to do this in New York and arranged to do it in the town of Ellenville, which is about twenty minutes from the Siddha Yoga Ashram in South Fallsburg, where Gurumayi was then in residence. Laura and I arranged to live in the ashram while I worked in the chiropractic office three days a week. This was the summer of 1992, and a month-long retreat was being held in the ashram. I was able to spend all my free time in the retreat, which was a true joy.

Two days before we left to go back to St. Louis, Gurumayi called us to a private meeting with her. She asked, "So what's next? Where will you practice?" We really didn't know at this point. We had driven around Pennsylvania and Virginia looking for a suitable location. I told her that we were considering somewhere near Philadelphia. She thought for a moment and then said, "I don't know if he needs someone, but you should meet Frank Gilbert while he is here." Frank was a chiropractor in New York City, and he came to the ashram regularly.

We came out of that meeting, and I was telling a friend what Gurumayi had said. He responded, "Well, there's Frank right now." He was in the hallway just a few yards away. I introduced myself, and we sat and spoke for a while. He said that he had been thinking of hiring an associate doctor, so the timing was good. Frank and I seemed to hit it off right away and so we made plans.

I told Gurumayi about this, and she approved. As Laura was now about five months pregnant with our second child, Gurumayi suggested that Laura live in the Siddha Yoga Ashram in South Fallsburg, while I stay in the ashram in Manhattan, work with Frank, and come up on weekends. She also knew, without my saying so, that New York City was a place where I really didn't want to live. I'd had my fill of New York City years before. Gurumayi said, "You can work with Frank there for a little while and then have your own clinic in a quieter place." Of course, we agreed.

First, Laura and I had to go back to St. Louis to tie up loose ends and attend my graduation ceremonies. I completed my studies over the next month and graduated *cum laude* on August 8, 1992. At the graduation ceremony, I noticed the date on the program and realized it was also the date of Bhagavan Nityananda's thirty-first *punyatithi*, the anniversary of the day he passed on. I also saw that I was in the 108th graduating class of Logan College. The number 108 is sacred in India. The synchronicity was not lost on me. My classmates had jokingly nominated me as the student most likely to have his chiropractic tables facing Mecca.

Having passed hundreds of class exams plus three rounds of National Board Exams, I still had to take the New York State Board exam. When I finally received my New York State chiropractic license I saw that my license number was 007108. James Bond (secret agent 007) came to mind as well as the sacred number 108 again. I knew I was on the right track.

1992: Graduating cum laude from Logan College of Chiropractic in St. Louis, Missouri.

28. A New Career Begins, 1992

Frank Gilbert and I became good friends. I assisted him in the office and lived in the Siddha Yoga Ashram in Manhattan, which was a twenty-minute walk to Frank's office in the San Remo building between 74th and 75th streets on Central Park West. This is an iconic, two-towered landmark building that is panned in just about every movie about New York City. Frank's office had a walk-in entrance, directly off the street, between the two towers. We started seeing patients at 7:30 a.m. I loved my early morning walks to the office as I saw all the shopkeepers getting ready for their day. I also passed by quite a few homeless people sleeping in doorways, which was a bit distressing and something I hadn't seen in New York City before.

I was very enthusiastic about applying my newly acquired skills. I felt prepared as a chiropractor, and I really enjoyed working with the patients. It was the culmination of years of hard work to get to this point. Frank was a good mentor. I learned a lot about patient care and saw why he was so successful. I would meditate every morning before work, and this was a great sustenance in dealing with the bustling city.

On weekends, I would make the one-and-a-half-hour drive to South Fallsburg. It was always a wonderful visit. Laura was happy there with a group of about five women who were all expecting babies around the same time. They had all become good friends. Gurumayi had assigned a devotee to look after all the expecting mothers. This was before cell phones existed, but pagers were in common use. Laura and I set up a series of codes so that she could page me should the need arise. Under our code, 333 meant, "Call me when you get a chance"; 222 meant, "Call me as soon as possible"; 111 meant, "Come now!" Laura's pregnancy was progressing nicely. She was well taken care of, and I knew I could be there in a short time if she needed me.

After a few months, Gurumayi invited Frank and his wife, Joko, to travel with her on tour to Japan and then on to Mexico. Frank hadn't been on a long vacation in many years, and he took this opportunity to be with Gurumayi. That gave me the opportunity to manage his practice by myself for about six weeks. I was thrilled as I could hone my skills and see what it was like to be in practice on my own. It went well; I felt competent that I could handle whatever came up.

By the third week of January, after Frank had returned, I got the call, "Come now!" It was time for our baby to be born. I left for South Fallsburg right away. Laura and I knew it was going to be close. The Northern Dutchess Hospital in Rhinebeck was an hour's drive from South Fallsburg. There was a wonderful birthing center there in an attached wing of the hospital. Laura and I had arranged for a midwife to assist as well as a supervising doctor. When we got there, the midwife estimated that Laura had a few hours yet before delivery. We took a room in a motel in Rhinebeck and stayed the night. The next day we returned to the birthing center and found that things had progressed well.

The miracle of childbirth took place, and Laura and I were very happy and relieved. The hospital staff knew the history of our earlier child's death, so they were being extra cautious. After a few hours, a doctor came in and said that he may have found something irregular in the baby's heart on an EKG and they wanted to have him evaluated at a neonatal intensive care unit about an hour away in Albany. The doctor said the ambulance was already on its way to transport him.

With obvious concern, I said that I needed to go with the baby, but the doctor explained that it was not going to be possible. I said, "Then we will check out of the hospital, and I would take him myself. I was not about to let this baby out of my sight."

The doctor replied that if I did that, the baby would not be admitted back to the hospital.

He wasn't pleased, but neither was I. Finally, I requested to talk to the ambulance company. I told them my situation and after assuring them that I was a doctor and that I was not going to be a disturbance to them, they agreed to let me come along.

So, away we went, with sirens blaring, to the pediatric wing of Albany Medical Center. When we got there the pediatrician on duty was surprised. He said emphatically, "Why is this child here? I told them that EKG was normal!" They apparently had read the EKG as if he were an adult and completely misinterpreted it. He said to take the baby home.

There was a problem, however. This was now no longer seen as an emergency, and there was no ambulance available to take us back to Rhinebeck. In the meantime, we were admitted to the neonatal care unit to wait. The hospital staff wanted to put the baby into a clear plastic crib that's used for emergency neonatal care. I couldn't bear to see my son in that sterile, cold-looking crib. After I described my situation, the nurses were very accommodating. They brought a rocking chair for me and let me sit there and hold the baby the whole time. They were very sympathetic and took good care of us; they even showed me how to change his diaper. I held him for the better part of nine hours before we were able to return to Laura back in Rhinebeck. What an adventure this was! Our first outing together!

*　　　*　　　*

Needless to say, Laura was very happy to have us back. Everything was good. Gurumayi sent us a large beautiful white teddy bear for the baby and shawls for both Laura and me. As is often the custom in India, a newborn child is given their name on the eleventh day after their birth. Gurumayi named him Joel, with a spiritual name of Jayaraj, a name meaning victorious king or triumphant lord. It is also an epithet for Ganesh, who represents strength and the overcoming of obstacles. I blissfully remained in the ashram for a few weeks and then returned to New York City and began the search for an apartment where we could all be together.

After a long search of very small and very expensive apartments, we learned of a friend who had recently married and was living upstate. Her former apartment on 93rd and Lexington on the Upper East Side of Manhattan was vacant. I looked at it and saw that it would work fine for us. We soon moved into her one-bedroom apartment and were very comfortable there.

My office was on the opposite side of Central Park from our apartment. I had to take a bus across the park on 86th Street and then walk down to 75th. Soon enough, winter set in. Having very little money at the time, I didn't really even have a proper winter coat. I wore only a London Fog raincoat that wasn't ever warm enough. I can remember many chilly mornings being quite cold on my way to the office. With the expense of the apartment and the new baby, I also had to defer my student loans for that first year. I did, however, learn a lot about patient management from the experience. These are the things that you can't possibly learn in school.

In retrospect, I also now realize that the experience of having lost our first child had made me a better doctor. I experienced compassion for people at a new and deeper level. Other than Baba I had never lost anyone close to me. I believe I carried that awareness throughout my career.

By the following summer, I began to feel that it was time to think about moving on. Gurumayi had originally told me that I would be in New York City for a while and then have my own clinic in a quieter place. On *Gurupurnima* of July 1993, as I approached Gurumayi on the darshan line, she said, "It's time." I knew exactly what she meant, and I felt ready. A few days later, I happened to pick up a chiropractic trade journal and saw a practice advertised for sale in Highland, New York, about an hour and a half north of the city. It was also about an hour's drive from the ashram in South Fallsburg. It sounded ideal. I called the owner and arranged to meet with him.

Dr. Nelson Peet and his wife, Dr. Helen Peet, had practiced together in the area for almost fifty years. Helen's father, Dr. John Killeen, was one of the first chiropractors in the Hudson Valley, having opened his office in 1910. Helen was one of the first female chiropractors in New York State. We hit it off nicely. Highland was a satellite office for them as they had sold their original practice in Newburgh to their son. They had intended to set up this office for their youngest daughter, who had just graduated from chiropractic college. She stayed for only six months and then decided she wanted to move to Georgia. It was too much for the Peets to manage the practice by themselves as they were ready to retire.

Highland was an ideal location for me as I wanted to be within easy driving distance of the ashram. The problem was that Dr. Peet wanted a total cash offer and that was well beyond my resources. I applied to a few banks for a loan, but as I was a new doctor without enough collateral, the banks were not willing to help. I went back and forth with Dr. Peet, but he held fast to his request for cash. After some time, I had to face the fact that it wasn't going to work.

About six weeks later, Laura, myself, and baby Joel were at the ashram in South Fallsburg, as had been our habit most weekends. Gurumayi was aware of our situation, and when we saw her in darshan, I updated her, telling her that the office in Highland wasn't going to happen. She slowly nodded. Immediately after the satsang, Laura and I took a coconut to the temple and offered it to Bhagavan Nityananda, now most often called Bade Baba, meaning "the elder Baba." We made our offering, and I mentally let the whole situation drop.

Only a few minutes later, we bumped into a friend from Hawaii whom Laura and I hadn't seen for quite a few years. This woman had spent time in the ashram in Honolulu and was also active with the Siddha Yoga meditation center on Kauai that I used to visit periodically. She asked what we had been doing, and I shared our story of the chiropractic practice we had been trying to buy. She said, "How much do you need?" I told her, and she said she had been looking for some new investments. She offered to loan us what amounted to half of what we needed at a fair interest rate.

As it had now been over six weeks since I had spoken to Dr. Peet, I had no idea if the practice was even still available. So, I called Dr. Peet to find out. He answered the phone in a very uncharacteristically jovial tone. Before I could say anything, he called out to his wife, "Oh Helen, Dr. Auerbach is on the phone!" He then said, "Dr. Auerbach, let me make this easy for you. My wife had a dream last night, and in the dream, God told her that you are the right person to buy the practice. So, I will personally finance half of the cost if you can come up with the rest." I now had the financing I needed. The two halves had come together most miraculously. I was, and still am, truly grateful. I felt surrounded by grace. We got to work drawing up all the necessary legal documents. I'm sorry I never asked Dr. Peet what God looked like in his wife's dream.

*   *   *

In December of 1993, our family moved to Highland, New York, and on January 28, 1994, I became the proud owner of Auerbach Family Chiropractic Center. Laura became the office manager, and we practiced there together for the next thirty years. Our son, Joel, was eleven months old at the time we began. He spent many days in his stroller at the office. A few years later, he was joined by his younger brother, David.

The night before the final closing of the office purchase, I had a dream. The office layout at the time was a series of rooms on either side of a long hallway with a closet at the far end. In my dream, at the end of the hallway, in place of the closet, was a full-length life-sized photo of Gurumayi. In the center of the hallway, was a fire pit just like the yajna pit used for the special fire ceremonies in Ganeshpuri. The message was clear: this was my offering to God and Guru. All day long I would go up one side of the hallway, down the other and back again in circles as I moved from room to room seeing my patients. This was my yajna, my offering. My work was my seva, my service.

During this time, I also joined the Highland Rotary Club. In 1994 I was invited to give a talk there and was then invited to be a member. Rotary International is the largest service organization in the world, present in more than two hundred countries with 1.4 million members. Rotary International even has an office at the United Nations. I felt that giving back to my community was an important part of my service as well. The Rotary motto is, "Service above self." That fit perfectly with my values, and I remained a member for the next twenty-nine years. I served as Rotary President in 1999 and 2000 and participated in many community projects during this time. Over the years I received numerous awards from the town, as well as the prestigious Rotary District Vocational Service Award. At times I was invited to speak at our meetings and was able to teach the group some basic meditation as well.

As usual, meditation was my sustenance. I would wake up by 5:15 a.m. and meditate for an hour before work each day. Such grace was with me. This is what allowed me to give my best to my patients. Some days I would arrive at the office in a state of great bliss. One morning while meditating, the form of a woman appeared to my lower right. There is no description of her that could contain her unearthly beauty. She radiated a divine presence that is beyond the ability of my memory to hold. She sat with both legs crossed to her right side. She smiled gently. She was the same Kundalini Devi who had handed me a red rose many years before. She radiated perfect innocence and purity. I felt blessed by her presence.

I worked very hard over the years in my office serving my patients. Often, I would see fifty to a hundred people in a day, and I had to address a variety of problems and conditions. The days were varied, and so were my meditations. On days when I had what seemed to be a shallow meditation, I longed for deeper connection even though I always knew that grace was still behind me. If a few days passed that way I would feel low energy and a bit down. How could I not long for these experiences? I knew that the universe was a manifestation of God, and. I wanted to immerse myself in that. Once Baba had told me not to crave meditation so much, but at times my longing for its depth was impossible to resist.

I remember a poem that I believe was written by a celebrated fourteenth-century Persian poet. I'm paraphrasing here as I can't find the original source:

> O Lord, I stand on the shore of your infinite ocean of love
> and throw myself in wholeheartedly.
> After a moment of bliss, a giant wave comes
> and throws me back onto the shore.
> O Lord, what is all this back and forth?

*　　　*　　　*

In 1996, our third son was born. Gurumayi named him David, with the spiritual name of Sundar, meaning beautiful. David was a great and joyful addition to the family. There was a relaxed atmosphere surrounding his birth, which was a welcome relief. I remember taking Joel to the hospital to meet his new brother. He was so excited to see his baby brother and held him with great love. When we presented David to Gurumayi, she held him and blessed him by sweetly and gently blowing her prana over his face. The two brothers were a good pair and grew close. As they got a bit older, we were able to send them both to the local Waldorf School, from the nursery level all the way to the eighth grade. I give a lot of credit to the Mountain Laurel Waldorf School in New Paltz for helping our two boys to become the wonderful, intelligent, thoughtful young men they are today.

For seven years after opening my practice, I visited the ashram in South Fallsburg to offer seva once a week. Then, after I got busier in the office, I continued once a month. This was very uplifting for me. Sometimes just driving there I would feel exquisite blissful energy flowing through me as I thought of the ashram and Gurumayi. As soon as I stepped inside, I was enveloped with an ecstatic sense of belonging and grace. I was so grateful that we were living close enough to do this. Laura and I also hosted a Siddha Yoga chanting and meditation group in our home for seventeen years. The group met twice a month with a wonderful community of people attending from throughout the Mid-Hudson Valley region. Laura and I put a lot of energy into this chanting and meditation group, and it was also a great source of fulfillment for us.

29. Wellness and Gratitude, 2014–24

Sometime in 2013, I connected with a chiropractor near Philadelphia who had developed a program called "8 Weeks to Wellness." I had known of his program for some time, but I wasn't yet ready for it. In more recent years, I began feeling that I needed to provide something more for my patients. I saw them getting out of pain, but I didn't see people changing their lifestyle enough to become truly healthy. What I did see was people gaining weight and developing diabetes and other lifestyle-based illnesses. I wanted to serve my community better by providing new resources and support. This program fit the bill.

After careful preparation, in September of 2014, Laura and I completely renovated our office and added a fitness training area and a massage room, and we also greatly expanded our nutritional programs and taught meditation. We hired fitness trainers and massage therapists. In addition to managing the office, Laura handled all the nutritional counseling. She became very proficient in managing weight loss programs. This venture was quite successful, and I was proud to be a part of it. We now became even busier with more people coming and going for all of our new programs.

By 2020, I began to contemplate what the exit plan would be for us. I was now in my seventies, and I began to think that I should consider selling the practice and retiring. I flirted with the idea for a while and put out some feelers. The COVID epidemic hit right around then, so it wasn't a great time to sell the practice.

In early 2023, I happened to connect with Dr. Dominic Rubino, a chiropractor who was interested in buying my practice. He had practiced in New York City for more than twenty years, and after moving to the Hudson Valley, wanted work that was closer to home. It was a compatible match, and he began working on his loans and other paperwork. Everything was moving along nicely.

It just so happened that at this time I needed to find a new personal physician for myself. My previous doctor, whom I had seen for the past thirty years for regular checkups, had just retired. I had had a nice rapport with him, and the two of us often discussed health topics. He sometimes had new doctors training with him. I remember him once telling a young doctor, "This is the healthiest seventy-year-old you will ever meet." I certainly felt healthy.

*   *   *

I did, however, need to find a new doctor for myself. After hesitating for about six months, on one particular day in my office, I heard from two different patients that a new doctor was nearby and that everyone was very happy with him. I set up a basic initial appointment to meet him. I had no symptoms at the time and was expecting an initial standard review. To my surprise when he listened to my heart and took my pulse, he began looking quite serious. I asked if everything was okay. He said, "Are you aware of how irregular your pulse is?"

I felt my own pulse then, and I perceived that there were multiple skipped heartbeats with long pauses in between and then rapid catchup beats. That's not good. The doctor did an EKG and was concerned about the results, so he sent me to a cardiologist right away.

The cardiologist said he thought this was probably just a "normal abnormal," but he ran some further tests: stress tests, nuclear stress tests, and CT scans. These showed that fifteen percent of my heartbeats were irregular, notably premature ventricular contractions; however, the actual final output of my heart, called ejection fraction, was within normal limits. The cardiologist still wasn't overly concerned. He said that up to ten percent of premature beats were fairly common, but as I now had fifteen percent, he recommended a catheterization procedure, just to be sure that nothing was being missed. He said that if they found some blockage, they might want to put in a stent or two. I agreed to the catheterization—but with some trepidation.

The day of the procedure came. I knew that, statistically speaking, there is a one percent chance of a stroke or some other heart event from undergoing this particular procedure. But I also knew that it would be foolish to refuse to have it done.

The physician took a route through my right arm to perform the catheterization. I was awake but lightly sedated. He wasn't in there for more than a few minutes when he ended the procedure. He said, "This is much more than we can address with a stent, you are going to need a triple bypass operation."

I was shocked. I had never had an invasive procedure of any kind prior to this and had never—in my entire life!—needed to take a prescription medication. He explained that the main artery to my heart, called the left main, was ninety percent blocked and that another artery on the left side was seventy percent blocked. He said there was also something else on the right that was blocked, but he hadn't been in long enough to evaluate this. He showed me the images. I could easily see the blockages.

I said to him, "But I have no symptoms. Just yesterday, I shoveled eight inches of snow from my driveway and did my neighbor's driveway as well. The day before that, I physically adjusted fifty patients in my office and felt nothing."

He looked at me intently and said, "You are a very fortunate man. If that last bit had clogged, you wouldn't have made it to the hospital alive in an ambulance." He called one of the heart surgeons to see me right away.

We spent an hour discussing the situation with the heart surgeon. He showed me the images from the catheterization and explained what needed to be done. I had taken and read many X-ray and MRI images over the years so I could easily see what he was showing me. It wasn't the famous left anterior descending artery (LAD) often referred to as the "widow maker." It was the left main, which feeds the LAD and is the primary artery to the heart, making it even more serious. He felt this was urgent, and so surgery was scheduled for the following week. He recommended that I not see any patients at all after that day.

I called Dr. Rubino, the chiropractor who was to take over my practice and told him what was going on. He was great about it. He said, "What do you need, Doc? Let me come into the practice now. I'll take all the patients, and we can work out the finances later." He really saved me. I don't know what I would have done if he hadn't been in the wings.

*   *   *

I had open-heart surgery on March 30, 2023, and we closed on the sale of the practice eight days later, on April 7. The synchronicity of these events was truly extraordinary. Once again, I felt that I was blessed to have everything come together like this. My only concern was that I wouldn't be there to say goodbye to my patients. I had been treating some of them for almost thirty years. In some families, that covered three generations. I had also looked forward to the six weeks of training and orientation sessions that I had discussed with Dr. Rubino. Fortunately, he was already a seasoned chiropractor.

After the procedure, the surgeon came in to tell me that he had only done a double bypass and that the third one he expected to do was one hundred percent blocked and calcified and therefore could not be bypassed. He said it looked like it had been that way for a very long time, perhaps decades. This was the right coronary artery, which is the main artery to the right side of the heart.

The surgeon then said, "The good news is that the blood vessels on the left side of your heart had grown many new blood vessels and that they were very large and full." This does happen. These are called collateral vessels. Essentially, the blood vessels on the left were supplying the right side of my heart. The surgeon added, "That happened because you took care of yourself over these years. You didn't gain weight, you kept active and exercised as you worked so hard for so long, and you also had a healthy attitude toward life. You basically gave yourself a natural bypass. That's why you weren't having symptoms." Then, pointing at me, he said, "You did that!"

At some point, I remembered that way back in 1971, when I was in Shree Gurudev Ashram, Baba asked a well-known cardiologist who was visiting to take me to Bombay for evaluation. I had become very thin. I did go with him. I stayed in a hospital for two nights and was released in apparent perfect health. In retrospect, I felt it curious that Baba had sent me with a cardiologist. Did Baba see something that was to be this future medical issue? Could something have begun developing that far back?

In fact, the surgeon told me that my right coronary artery had been blocked for decades, possibly due to a "silent heart attack" years before. I still wonder about this.

*   *   *

The recovery from the surgery was long and quite extensive. After five days in the hospital, I came home and had to sleep in a recliner for about six weeks. I was advised not to sleep on my side for twelve weeks due to the wires that had been placed on my sternum to close it and the recliner was the easiest way to do this. When I finally had the strength to climb the stairs to my bedroom, it was a tremendous relief to sleep in my own bed.

At some point early in my recovery, there was a live video stream with Gurumayi from Shree Muktananda Ashram. Swami Ishwarananda called me to make sure I was aware of the satsang. As soon as I was logged on, Gurumayi looked right into the camera and said, as if she were speaking directly to me, "This is the time to let go of all roles and responsibilities. It's all about the heart, the heart, the heart." This was clearly very meaningful to me. The perfect message for the perfect time.

I progressed from a walker to a cane and then finally was able to walk independently. I was then given thirty-six visits of cardiac rehab at the hospital which was a big boost to my energy. After completing that, I joined the local gym and have kept it up at least three days a week since. In between days, I walk two to five miles. Now, after more than one year, I am just about one hundred percent back to normal.

I remember one day, back in the early 1990s, when Laura and I had gone to offer seva in the ashram in South Fallsburg. After satsang, we went up in darshan to see Gurumayi, and she said to me, "When will you write your book?" At the time, I felt it was something that she seemed to know would be done someday. I sat down that very weekend and tried to write a bit. It was hard to follow up, however, as I was working ten-hour days, five days a week, and my weekends were filled with family time and household chores. It has been on my mind all these years since. Now, that I had a lot of free time during my recovery, I began to focus on my writing.

The fruit of that effort is this book.

* * *

In looking back on my life, I recognize the amazing influence of grace throughout. I am exceedingly grateful for having had the opportunity to spend so much time with two such amazing beings as Baba Muktananda and Gurumayi Chidvilasananda. It is such a rare opportunity to be with beings like them. True gurus are not at all common. I have met quite a few great beings in my life, but for me there is no one like Baba or Gurumayi. They have given so much to this world. To say that my life has been enriched by them is a massive understatement. I have witnessed thousands of others who have been awakened and supported in their spiritual endeavors. The positive transformation in my life has been nothing short of a miracle.

My meditation continues to deepen and unfold—and I continue to blossom upward. Having seen the pathway to the highest experience of my own divinity, I can now include all life experience within that vision. I do still continue to long for complete union, although it is clear that it is only a matter of grace for that vision to stabilize. As I move more and more deeply within that experience, the small "I" of my personal self often merges into the pure light of existence itself. I can see that the infinite freedom and ecstasy of the divine spills over as the infinite ecstasy of the manifestation of this entire universe. They are one and the same and have never been separate. The world itself is not inert matter. It is totally alive, pure conscious awareness. It is God's infinite being.

Recently, as I sat down to prepare for meditation, I looked up at a photo of Bhagavan Nityananda and saw a beautiful soft glow emanating from it. I looked over at my favorite photo of Baba Muktananda and saw the same divine glow. I looked at Gurumayi's photo and once again it emanated a beautiful radiance. I then felt my own heart filling with radiance.

I saw that the radiance in my gurus and in myself is the same. I felt merged in that light. My essence is only that light of pure radiance. I am completely fulfilled in that space. I cannot distinguish that light from any concept I have ever had of God. My nature is pure existence, pure awareness, and pure ecstasy.

GLOSSARY

ASHRAM: A place of retreat, where residents engage in spiritual practice and study scriptural teachings.

DARSHAN: Being in the presence of a holy person; seeing a holy person.

GURU: A spiritual master.

LINGAM: A symbol of the formless form of the Hindu deity Lord Shiva.

KUNDALINI: The goddess Kundalini (Kundalini Devi); the latent, innate spiritual power in a human being which can be awakened by a transmission of energy from a Siddha guru.

MURTI: A representation of a chosen deity that has been enlivened by worship.

PUJA: Worship; actions that constitute an act of worship.

SADHANA: The spiritual path; disciplined spiritual practice.

SANNYASA: Monkhood; monastic vows.

SATSANG: A gathering of spiritual seekers for the purpose of chanting, meditation, and listening to inspirational teachings.

SEVA: Selfless service; work offered on behalf of the Guru.

SHAKTIPAT: The initiation by which the guru transfers the divine shakti (energy) that brings about an awakening of Kundalini in a seeker. This initiation can happen through the guru's touch, intention (*sankalpa*), or by seeing the guru's form or even just a photograph of the guru.

SIDDHA YOGA: The spiritual path directed by Gurumayi Chidvilasananda and founded by her guru, Swami Muktananda.

ACKNOWLEDGEMENTS

I was inspired to write this book to express the depth of gratitude I feel for Baba Muktananda and Gurumayi Chidvilasananda, the two *siddha* gurus who transformed my life. I offer every word I have written at their feet. My life has been enhanced beyond measure by their grace.

The book began to take form as I was recovering from open-heart surgery. It was a contemplative time, and I found myself wondering where my awareness had been while I had lain unconscious on the operating table with my chest opened up. For a few weeks this question was persistently on my mind.

Then one night, I had a dream. At first, it was like a scene from the Indian epic *Ramayana* in which there is a classic story involving Hanuman, the monkey god who was a great devotee and friend of Lord Rama. I was watching this story unfold in my dream—Rama was offering Hanuman a beautiful pearl necklace for the great service he had rendered, and Hanuman was refusing the Lord's gift. Hanuman told the Lord, "What do I need with material things? You are inscribed in my heart forever!" To prove his words, Hanuman ripped open his chest and revealed that the image of Lord Rama was, indeed, installed right there on his heart. In my dream, I then saw myself on the operating table with my chest opened up—Baba's image was on my open heart.

Then I knew where my awareness had been. I had been with Baba the whole time.

I had the space, then, to write the book I had known for a quarter of century that I must write as a way to record my gurus' greatness.

No book is created without the assistance of a multitude of people, and everyone who played a role in this endeavor has my sincere appreciation. First, without the love and support of my wife, Laura, my story would never have been written. I am truly grateful for her patience regarding the long hours I spent writing, as well as her thoughtful input as it progressed.

I am also grateful to my editor, Margaret Bendet, who appears in the book as Peggy Bendet and Mahananda. Whatever name she goes by, she was thorough and professional, and she enormously enhanced the clarity of my stories. The beautiful front cover photograph was provided by TJ (Devadatta) Best. The artful layout was designed by Laura Duggan of Nicasio Press.

A debt of gratitude is due to the SYDA Foundation for their support in this endeavor.

ABOUT THE AUTHOR

Here, Steven Auerbach is with his immediate family—his wife, Laura, and their two amazing sons, Joel (left, thirty-one) and David (twenty-seven).

Steven Auerbach and his wife, Laura, have been happily married for forty years and have two grown sons. In his teens, Steve led a campus protest. In his twenties, he followed an Indian holy man, receiving an inner awakening and living in ashrams across the US and in India. Before he was thirty, he took vows of monkhood and was given the monastic name Swami Sadananda, which means "ever blissful." Seven years later, without leaving his spiritual path or dropping the daily practices of meditation and service, Steve embarked on another phase of life in which, ultimately, he married, had children, finished college, and became a doctor of chiropractic. Now retired after more than three decades as a successful chiropractor, Steve writes about this journey in which he continues to integrate his life with a deep spiritual understanding.

www.ingramcontent.com/pod-product-compliance
Lightning Source LLC
Chambersburg PA
CBHW051512120626
46551CB00012B/892